Beginning Guitar
For Adults
The Grown-Up Approach to Playing Guitar

Copyright©MCMXCIX Workshop Arts, Inc.
All rights reserved. Printed in USA

Acquisition and editorial: Nathaniel Gunod
Music typesetting: Joe Bouchard
Recorded at Bar None Studios, Northfield, CT
Cover Photo: BP&V Photographic Associates
Cover and internal design: Cathy C. Bolduc
Fender Guitar courtesy of East Coast Music Mall, Danbury, CT
Acoustic guitar courtesy of David Smolover
"Jake,"(Golden Retriever) courtesy of Mark Dutton
Special thanks to Leo Valcourt & Louisette Bolduc for the use of their home.

Book: ISBN 1-929395-00-0
Book and CD: ISBN 1-929395-01-9
CD: ISBN 1-929395-06-X

Nick Vecchio

Contents

About the Author 4
Introduction 5

Chapter One — 6

Getting Started 6
    Buying Your Guitar 6
    Amplifiers 7
    Parts of the Guitar 8
    Holding the Guitar 9
    Left-Hand Technique 10
    Right-Hand Technique 11
    The Guitar Strings: Names and Numbers 12
    Tuning Your Guitar 13
    Relative Tuning 14

Chapter Two — 15

Lesson 1: Chords 15
    Reading Chord Diagrams 15
    The G Chord 15
Lesson 2: Basic Reading 16
Lesson 3: Strumming Chords in Time 17
Lesson 4: Quarter Notes 18
Lesson 5: Two Songs 19
Lesson 6: Half Notes 20
Lesson 7: Whole Notes 21
Lesson 8: Three New Chords 22
Lesson 9: Strumming Rhythms 23
Lesson 10: Eighth-Note Strums 24
Lesson 11: Putting It All Together 25
Lesson 12: Your First Full Songs 27
    Be on My Side 27
    Let Me In 27

Chapter Three — 28

Lesson 1: Tablature (TAB) 28
Lesson 2: Standard Music Notation 30
Lesson 3: Notes on the 1st String 31
    Quarter-Note Rest 31
Lesson 4: Notes on the 2nd String 32
    Half-Note Rest 32
Lesson 5: The 1st and 2nd Strings Combined .. 33
    It's a Good Life 33
    Dance on a Rope 33
Lesson 6: Notes on the 3rd String 34
    Octaves 34
    Whole-Note Rest 34
Lesson 7: Notes on the 1st, 2nd and 3rd Strings .. 35
    The Fermata 35
    Taking a Walk 35
Lesson 8: Notes on the 4th String 36
Lesson 9: Notes on the 1st, 2nd, 3rd
         and 4th Strings 37
    Mix-Ins 37
Lesson 10: Notes on the 5th String 38
    Ledger Lines 38
    The Final Double Bar 39
Lesson 11: Ties and Accidentals 40
    Ties 40
    Accidentals 40
    Sharp Suit, Nice Tie 41
Lesson 12: Notes on the 6th String 42
    Hitting On All Six 43
Lesson 13: Chords Written in TAB
          and Standard Notation 44

Chapter Four — 45

Lesson 1: New Chords—A, D and E 45
Lesson 2: Eighth-Note Rest 46
    Buffetville 48
    Crazy Girl 50
Lesson 3: Reggae Accompaniment Rhythm 51
    Reggae Tune 51
Lesson 4: New Chords—F and G7 52
    The F Chord Barre 52
    You Can Usually Get What You Need 52
    The G7 Chord 53
Lesson 5: Musical Road Maps 54
    Twisted 55

Chapter Five 56

Lesson 1: Flatpicking Arpeggios 56
   Dark, Cloudy Day 57
   Great This Evening 58
Lesson 2: Bass-Strum Technique 60
   Country Blues 61
Lesson 3: Slash Chords and Muting 62
   Slash Chords 62
   Muting 62
   Rockin' Rodent 63
Lesson 4: Root-5th Strum Technique 64
   Waltzing My Baby 65
   Let's Party 66

Chapter Six 68

Lesson 1: Fingerstyle—Thumb vs. Fingers 68
   Lost Love 69
Lesson 2: Fingerstyle—Thumb and Fingers 70
   House Cat Dreaming 70
Lesson 3: Fingerstyle Roots and 5ths 71
Lesson 4: Life Beyond the 3rd Fret 72
   The Rain in Spain 72

Chapter Seven 74

Lesson 1: New Chords—A7 and E7 74
Lesson 2: New Chord—C7 75

Chapter Eight 76

Lesson 1: The Blues 76
   The Twelve-Bar Blues Progression 76
Lesson 2: Playin' the Blues 77
Lesson 3: Eighth-Note Triplets 78
Lesson 4: Swing Eighth Notes 79
   Swing It! 79
Lesson 5: Blues Pattern #1 80
Lesson 6: Blues Pattern #2 82
Lesson 7: A New Blues Rhythm 84
Lesson 8: A New Chord—D Minor 85
Lesson 9: A Classic Blues Riff 86
Lesson 10: A New Chord—B7 87
Lesson 11: Cool Blues Articulation 88
   Eric's Boogie 89
Lesson 12: Three Minor 7 Chords—Amin7,
      Dmin7 and Emin7 90

Chapter Nine 91

Lesson 1: Moveable Chords 91
Lesson 2: Root-6 Barres 92
Lesson 3: Root-5 Barres 94

A compact disc is available for this book. This disc can make learning with the book easier and more enjoyable. The symbol shown above will appear next to every example that is on the CD. Use the CD to help insure that you are capturing the feel of the examples, interpreting the rhythms correctly, and so on. The track numbers below the symbols correspond directly to the example you want to hear. Track 1 will help you tune your guitar to this CD.

Have fun!

About the Author

Nick Vecchio

Massachusetts-born Nick Vecchio has been providing guitar and bass instruction since 1988. A graduate of the Berklee College of Music, Nick has been performing regularly since his late teens. He currently teaches and administrates for The National Music Workshop, a division of The National Guitar Workshop.

Acknowledgements

Thank you to Dave Smolover and Nat Gunod for all the opportunities. Thank you to my wife Christine, my mother Josephine and the rest of my family for always encouraging me.

Dedication

This book is dedicated to the memory of my father, Carmen A. Vecchio, who I'm sure would have been proud.

Welcome to *Beginning Guitar for Adults*. I'm glad you have chosen the guitar as your instrument. Thanks for choosing this book to help get you started.

This book and the other two books in this series—
Rock Guitar for Adults and *Blues Guitar for Adults*—makes certain assumptions:

1. As an adult, you have a busy, stressful life and want your guitar education to be enjoyable, painless and direct. You don't want a lot of preliminaries. You want to get right to it.

2. You're pretty smart. You're not new to life, your just new to the guitar.

This book focuses on the most important aspect of guitar: playing songs! Why else would you want to play a musical instrument? The book you are now holding in your hands starts you off with chords and songs in a variety of styles—folk, reggae, rock and blues. I say, "Get on the fast track."

You should be consistent in your practice habits. Play a little every day and a lot whenever you can. Use this book in the order it is presented and you will get where you want to go quickly. Then, keep the ball rolling and pick up Rock Guitar for Adults and/or Blues Guitar for Adults.

Enjoy!

GETTING STARTED

So you've finally decided to play the guitar. Congratulations! You're entering a new world of fun and relaxation. Buying your first guitar should be a pleasant experience but there are decisions to make.

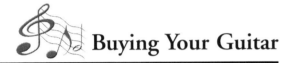

Buying Your Guitar

ACOUSTIC OR ELECTRIC?

The first decision is whether to play an acoustic or electric guitar. Some people feel that a beginner should start with an acoustic guitar. This is not necessarily true. You should have a guitar that inspires you—one that you will enjoy.

The best way to decide this is to think about your favorite artist or music. If you tend to lean more towards Bob Dylan or James Taylor, then you probably want a folk guitar (steel-string acoustic). For classical or flamenco style music, such as the music of Paco De Lucia, then you want a classical guitar (nylon-string acoustic). For rock, blues or jazz, you want an electric guitar.

Electric guitars come in many styles and shapes. They have many different sound qualities, and again, the guitar you choose will depend on the type of music you prefer. Typically, a blues fan would like a Fender Stratocaster (a "Strat"). A rock lover can go with a Strat also, but should consider a Gibson Les Paul for its thicker tone. A jazz lover could go with either of the above, and would also consider a hollow-body electric such as a Gibson L-5, which has a nice mellow tone.

Go to the nearest reputable dealer and shop. If you have a guitarist friend or have already found a teacher, bring them along or ask their advice. Have the sales person demonstrate the guitar for you. Tell them the type of music you are interested in and look for the best sounding guitar for that style. When you think you have found the guitar you are looking for, hold it and try pressing the strings against the fingerboard yourself. This should be easy. The strings should not be hard to push down.

You do not have to pay a lot of money to get a decent guitar. Find the one you like and buy it if the price is good for you. If it's too expensive, you have two options: try to haggle with the salesperson, or explain your situation and ask if you can try something comparable for less money. Some salespeople are paid on commission, so keep that in mind when looking for the best deal.

Make sure that the dealer has a repair, return or exchange policy. This is very important whether you are buying a used or new instrument.

If you love the sound of an acoustic guitar, by all means get one. If what you want to do is to rock out, there is no reason not to go buy an electric guitar—right now!

Amplifiers

If you have decided to go the electric route, you will need an amplifier ("amp"). Most amplifiers are appropriate for a specific style of music. Again, your choice will depend on what type of music you are interested in playing.

Go to your nearest reputable dealer and ask the salesperson for their advice. Low-powered, inexpensive amplifiers are available. (The power of an amp is not always related to its physical size, so check out the "specs.") This kind of amp will be useful for practice or for playing with another guitarist. If you intend to start jamming with a full band—including a drummer—a low-powered amp will not be adequate. The less powerful the amp, the less options will be available to you. You should also make sure that the amplifier has distortion (that crunchy sound found in lots of rock), a clean sound (for smoother kinds of music) and reverb (echo).

All amplifiers should have some type of equalization ("E.Q."). Just like a home stereo, "high end" or "treble" boosts or cuts the upper frequencies and makes the sound brighter; "midrange" ("mid") boosts or cuts the middle frequencies; and "low end" ("bass") boosts or cuts the low frequencies.

Pickups are located on the body of the guitar just under the strings. They magnify the sound and relay it to the amplifier. There are two basic types of pickups: single coil, which give a thinner, honkier sound (found on Fender Strats); and humbuckers, which give a thicker, beefier sound (found on Gibson Les Pauls).

If you chose the acoustic route, there are also ways to amplify the sound. You have two choices: You can buy an acoustic pickup, which is available at any music store and can be taken in and out at will, or you can buy an acoustic guitar with the pickup built in (most of these need a battery to power the pickup). The latter choice is preferable for most players. Either way, you will need to buy an amp. There are several brands out there specifically for acoustic guitars but they tend to be expensive. A regular amp will be sufficient.

TWO CLASSIC GUITAR AMPLIFIERS

The Fender Twin Reverb

The Marshall Half-Stack

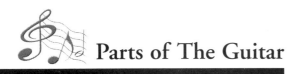

Parts of The Guitar

OPEN G
6 D
5 G
4 D
3 G
2 B
1 D

ACOUSTIC GUITAR **ELECTRIC GUITAR**

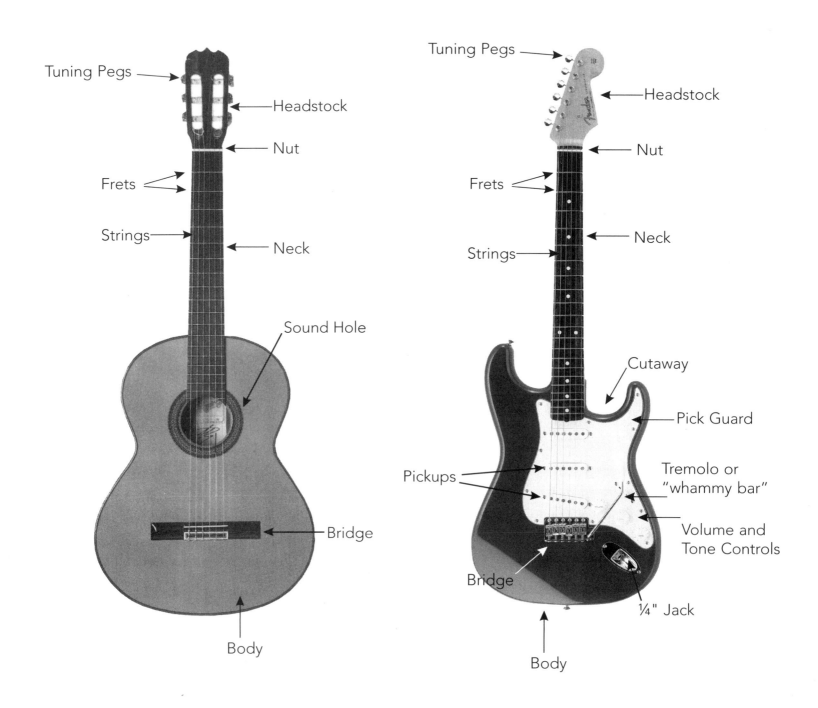

Chapter One

Holding the Guitar

The most important thing to remember is that the guitar should feel comfortable, like an extension of your body. Make sure the neck of the guitar points upwards toward the ceiling so you have access to the entire neck.

There are three basic positions:

1. Seated with or without a strap. Keep the neck in an upward position. Thish is the optimum playing position. This allows for full access to the full range f the neck.

2. Seated with your left foot elevated. The guitar rests between your legs with your left knee elevated. You can buy a guitar footstool for this purpose. If you do not have a footstool, anything that raises your foot about six inches will do.

3. Standing. A strap is necessary with this position and will keep the neck in an upward position.

 Left-Hand Technique

The job of the left hand is to press the strings at the appropriate frets in order to produce the desired tones.

THE LEFT-HAND FINGERS
The fingers are indicated as follows:

Index .... 1, 1st finger
Middle .... 2, 2nd finger
Ring .... 3, 3rd finger
Pinky .... 4, 4th finger

THE POSITION
Your thumb should be around the back of the neck of the guitar, pointing upward behind your middle finger.

When playing a single note or chord, your fingers should be arched so the notes are being played by your fingertips. This prevents your fingers from accidentally interfering with or touching another string.

Place your fingers just to the left of the frets. Do not play with your fingers directly on the fret wire. Placing fingers too far to the left of the fret may cause buzzes or muted notes.

Your wrist should be bent towards the floor. Your palm should not touch the neck of the guitar.

Trim your left-hand fingernails. You can't play guitar if the nails on your left hand are too long.

Chapter One

Right-Hand Technique

The right hand is just as important as the left hand. The right hand drives the left hand and provides the rhythm for the song.

Most guitarists play with a pick unless they play fingerstyle, which will be discussed later in this book.

For now, it is recommended that you use a pick. Hold it firmly between your thumb and index finger as pictured to the right.

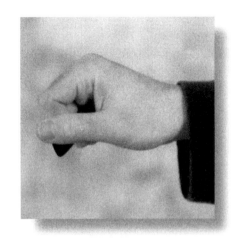

STRUMMING

The first action your right hand will perform is called a *strum*. A strum is performed by moving the tip of the pick swiftly across the strings. Sometimes, you will strum all six strings. At other times, you may only strum the top four or five strings.

You can strum two ways:

1. With a downstroke (towards the floor)
2. With an upstroke (towards the ceiling).

This is the symbol for a downstroke:

This is the symbol for an upstroke:

Here's a Tip...
Do not strum using your whole arm. Instead, try to move from your wrist.

The Guitar Strings: Names and Numbers

In this diagram, the guitar is shown standing vertically. The vertical lines represent the strings and the horizontal lines represent the frets. The string farthest to the right is the 1st string, E. It has the highest *pitch* (degree of highness or lowness of a musical sound). The string farthest to the left is the 6th string, E. It has the lowest pitch. You may have noticed that both the 1st and 6th strings are called E. The difference between them is that they are two *octaves* apart. Octave is the word used to describe the closest distance between any two notes with the same name. High E and low E both sound like E—but one is in a high range and the other is in a low range.

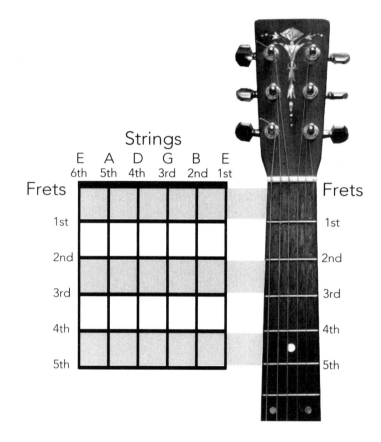

John Hendershott, 42
President of communications company

"Since I was a kid, I wanted to play guitar but did not have the time. I reached a point where a decision had to be made and the decision was— *I will make the time for music and I will realize my dream of being able to play music for my wife, daughter and friends.—* So far, it's working out."

Tuning Your Guitar

It is very important to make sure the guitar is in tune before each practice session. There are a variety of ways this can be done. The traditional method is to tune by ear. This is called *relative tuning*. To do this, you need only purchase a tuning fork to give you a starting pitch.

A tuning fork will give you one pitch—either E (to tune the 6th string) or A (to tune the 5th string). From there, you tune on your own. (see Relative Tuning, page 14).

Some people use a pitch pipe, which gives a pitch to match for each string.

The pitch pipe has six individual pipes that correspond to the strings on the guitar. Just blow into the pipe and match the corresponding string to the sound.

Alternatively, you can purchase an electronic tuning device. They can be bought for between $30 and $80 in most music stores. This is probably your best choice, since it is easy and will train your ear, although everyone should eventually learn relative tuning.

An electric tuner will read a pitch and tell you if it is sharp (high) or flat (low).

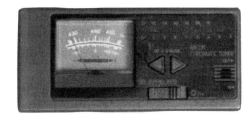

Chapter One

# Relative Tuning

Relative tuning is otherwise known as "tuning by ear." This is the most common and traditional method.

 If you have the CD that is available for this book, you can tune your guitar to Track 1.

Track 1

1) First, you need to find a reference pitch—either from a tuning fork, a piano or another guitar. Use this to tune your 6th (lowest) string, E.

2) Press the 6th at 5th fret of the with your left hand. Tune the open* 5th string to this pitch.

3) Press the 5th string at the 5th fret. Tune the open 4th string to this pitch.

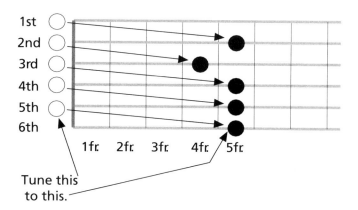

4) Press the 4th string at the 5th fret. Tune the open 3rd string to this pitch.

5) Press the 3rd string at the 4th fret. Tune the open 2nd string to this pitch.

6) Press the 2nd string at the 5th fret. Tune the open 1st string to this pitch.

Lesson.....

* An open string is the note that is produced when you pluck a string with your right hand without fingering a note with your left hand.

Chapter Two

LESSON 1: CHORDS

A *chord* is three or more notes played simultaneously. Remember, this is your first step in playing guitar—be patient and practice regularly. Before long, it will be easy!

Reading Chord Diagrams

Chord diagrams show us where to place our fingers to play a chord. The chord diagram at right shows a G chord. The vertical lines represent the strings. The horizontal lines are the frets. The string on the far left is the 6th string. The black dots show where to place your fingers. The numbers at the top of the diagram represent the fingers used by your left hand. An "0" at the top of the diagram means "open string," and that string should be included in the strum. An "X" means that the string should *not* be played.

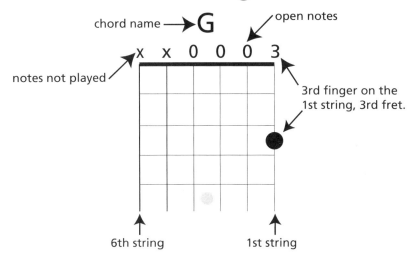

The G Chord

Here are two types of "G" Chords. You can use either one, but try to use the G2 version if you can.

G-1: 3rd Finger, 3rd Fret, 1st String

Strum from the 4th string down towards the floor.

G-2: 2nd Finger, 3rd Fret, 6th String.
1st Finger, 2nd Fret, 5th String.
3rd Finger, 3rd Fret, 1st String.

Strum from the 3rd string down towards the floor.

D7: 1st Finger, 1st Fret, 2nd String.
2nd Finger, 2nd Fret, 3rd String.
3rd Finger, 2nd Fret, 1st Sting.

Strum from the 4th string down towards the floor.

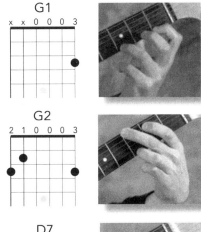
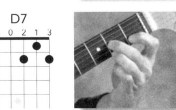

PRACTICE METHOD

Memorize each chord.

When you can play each chord, go from one chord to the next as fast as you can without looking at the diagrams. Concentrate and watch your fingers move from chord to chord.

Notice that when moving from G to D7, the 3rd finger should slide down the neck one fret. Attempt this without picking up the 3rd finger.

LESSON 2: BASIC READING

A time signature is a set of two numbers that appears at the beginning of every piece of music. It tells us how the musical time is organized. Most of the music we listen to is in 4/4 time, or *common time* **C**. This means that the music appears in groups of four *beats*. A beat is similar to a pulse, which is consistent with the ticking of a clock or *metronome* (a musical timing device which provides consistent beats at varying speeds). Think of the beat as the heartbeat of the music.

You will find the time signature at the beginning of a *staff*, which is a group of five lines and four spaces. These lines and spaces will become important to us later, as we learn to read and play melodies. Just before the time signature there is a *treble clef*, which is always found in guitar music. This will also be very important to note reading.

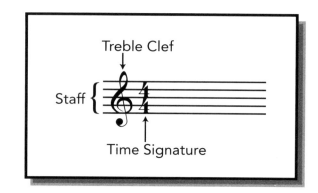

Each group of four beats is called a *measure*. Measures are marked with *bar lines*.

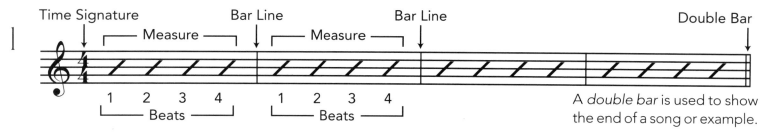

A *double bar* is used to show the end of a song or example.

There are many possible time signatures. For example: 3/4, which means three beats per measure, is another popular time signature.

NOTE:
Listening is a major part of learning to play the guitar. Select and play your favorite musical recording. Tap your foot to the beat. You will find that most music is in 4/4 time.

Chapter Two

LESSON 3: STRUMMING CHORDS IN TIME

This is where we apply the element of time to strumming chords.
In other words, here's where we start making music!

With your pick or thumb, strum down vertically across the strings four times in each measure. The chord to play is indicated above the staff. Keep playing the indicated chord until a new chord appears. For example, begin with a G chord and continue strumming (a total of two measures, or eight beats) until the D7 appears.

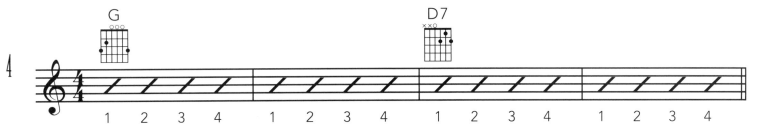

With your pick or thumb, strum down vertically across the strings three times per measure.

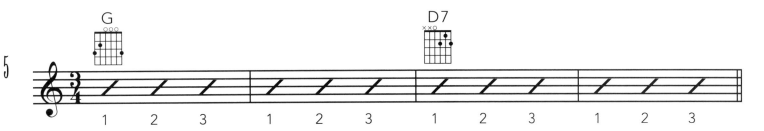

NOTE:
Remember, you have a choice between two types of G chords: G1 or G2 (page 15).

Chapter Two

LESSON 4: QUARTER NOTES

One strum per beat is shown with a *quarter note* which for now is written as a slash with a stem:

This is a *repeat symbol*. This means to return to the beginning and play again. In the case of an exercise, assume that it means to repeat many times.

This is the symbol for a *down-stroke*:

Play example 6 to practice reading the notation for quarter-note strums.

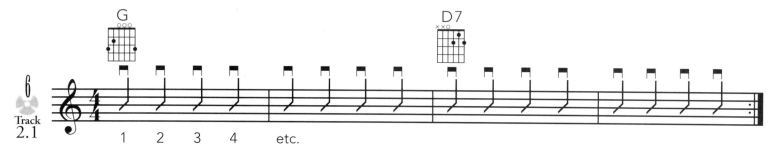

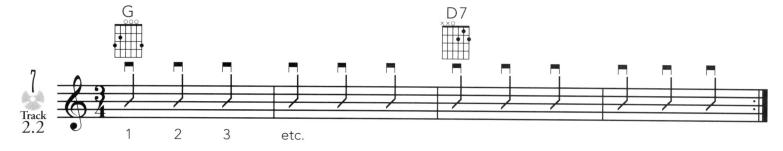

"I play guitar for fun. It also helps stimulate the gray matter between my ears. I like blues and rock the most but enjoy all aspects of music."

Jack Thrasher, 57
Road Construction Engineer Technician

LESSON 5: TWO SONGS

This is an *up-stroke* symbol. It indicates bringing your pick or thumb in an upwards motion across the strings:

Have fun strumming through these songs. Practice slowly until you gain confidence.

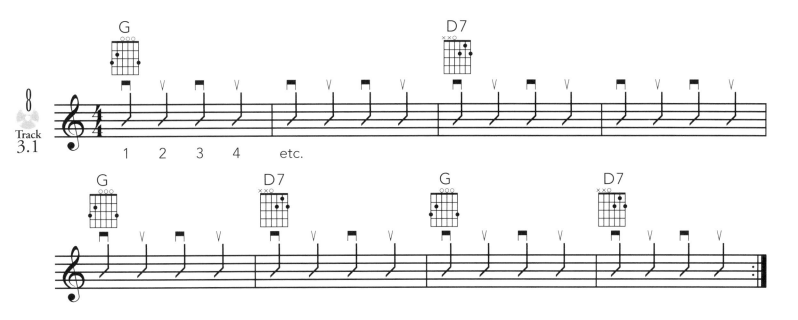

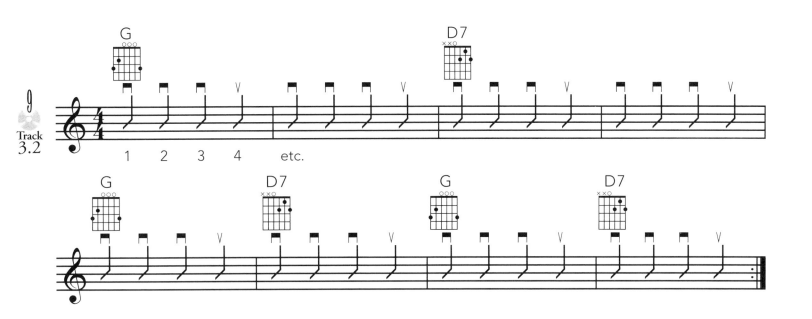

LESSON 6: HALF NOTES

Half-note strums are two beats in duration and are displayed as a diamond shape with a stem:

Below is an example showing two measures of half notes. Since a half note equals two beats, you can play two of them in each measure.

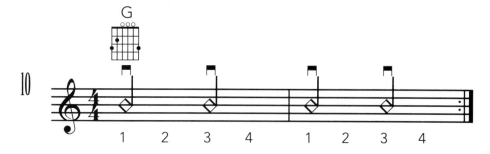

Notice that the half note is played on beats 1 and 3:

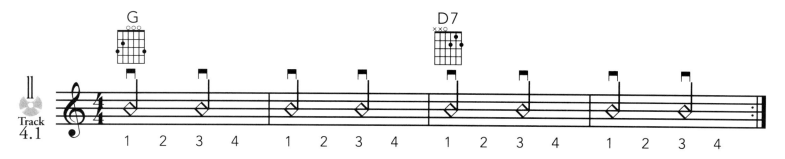

As you know, there are three beats per measure in $\frac{3}{4}$ time. A half note takes up two of the beats. A quarter note will occupy beat 3. Notice the down-up strumming pattern:

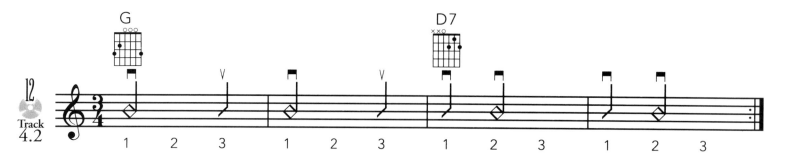

LESSON 7: WHOLE NOTES

A *whole note strum* is four beats in duration and is shown as a diamond shape with no stem:

A whole note is struck on beat 1 of the measure and lasts the whole measure:

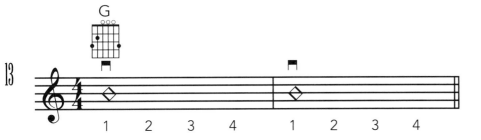

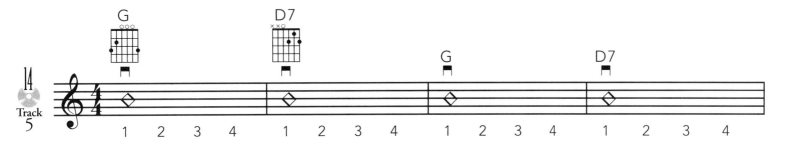

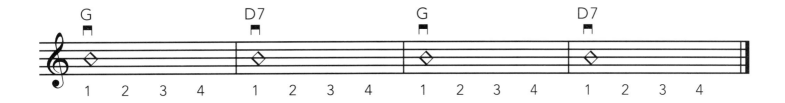

Make sure you are comfortable with the G and D7 chords before continuing. It's always best to master each step before taking the next.

LESSON 8: THREE NEW CHORDS

You are surely ready for some new chords. The C Major, A Minor and E Minor chords should provide the challenge you seek.

C MAJOR (C)

3rd finger, 3rd fret, 5th string
2nd finger, 2nd fret, 4th string
1st finger, 1st fret, 2nd string

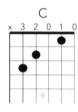 

A MINOR (Amin)

2nd finger, 2nd fret, 4th string
3rd finger, 2nd fret, 3rd string
1st finger, 1st fret, 2nd string

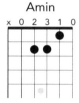 

E MINOR (Emin)

1st finger, 2nd fret, 5th string
2nd finger, 2nd fret, 4th string

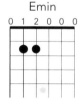 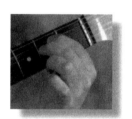

Notice the sound quality of the minor chords (Amin and Emin) as opposed to C and G, which are major chords. The minor chords sound sad or dark compared to the major chords, which sound happy or bright. As you advance and learn a little about basic music theory, you will see that there are important differences between major and minor chords that cause these differences in sound.

Here's a Tip...

Notice that when changing from C to Amin you need only move your 3rd finger from the 5th string to the 3rd. The 1st and 2nd fingers stay where they are. Also, notice that the 2nd finger on the 2nd fret of the 4th string is common to all three chords. You can pivot on this finger as you change between C, Emin and Amin.

Here is an exercise to try your new chords:

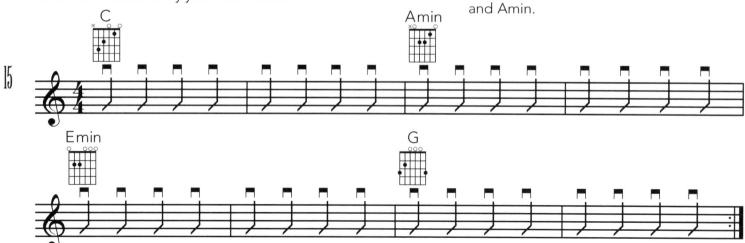

LESSON 9: STRUMMING RHYTHMS

Life in the music world would get dull if we didn't vary the rhythms. Below are two songs that mix quarter, half and whole notes to create different rhythms. Focus on playing with a steady beat. You'll also get a chance to mix the five chords you know. Have fun!

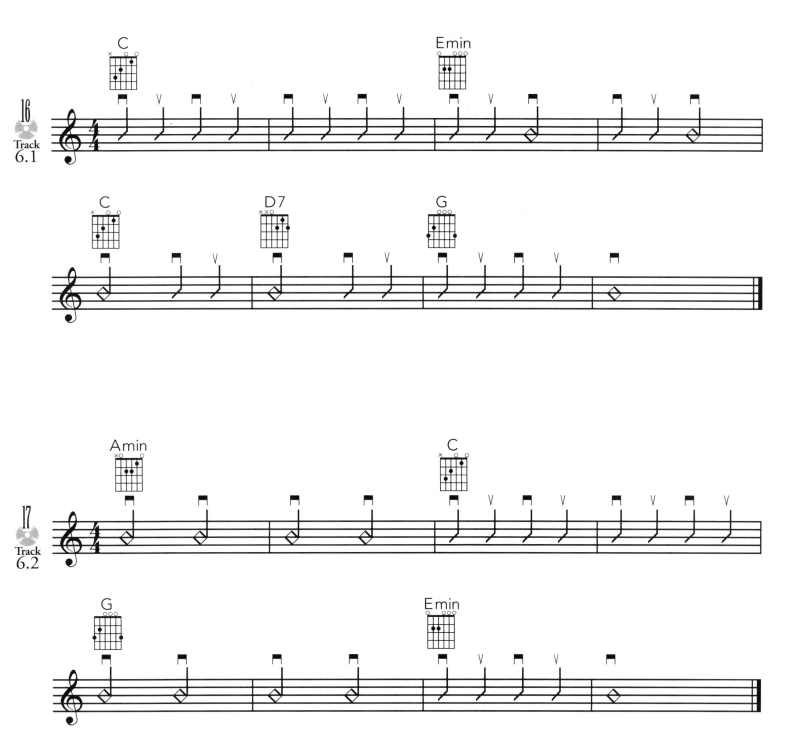

LESSON 10: EIGHTH-NOTE STRUMS

So far, you have learned these strum values:

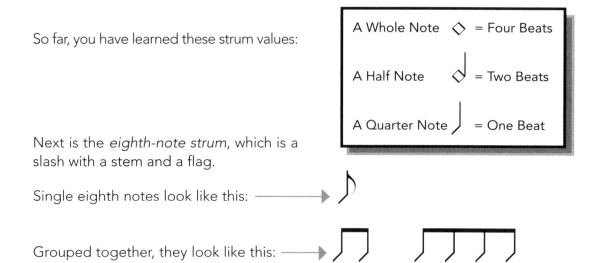

Next is the *eighth-note strum*, which is a slash with a stem and a flag.

Single eighth notes look like this: ⟶ ♪

Grouped together, they look like this: ⟶ ♫ ♬

Eighth notes last for half of a beat. In other words, you can play two eighth notes in each beat.

Try this:
Play quarter notes (one note per beat) tapping your foot and counting aloud: "1, 2, 3, 4." Observe that your foot hits the floor *on* the beats. Now try tapping your foot and saying "1 & 2 & 3 & 4 &." Play along, strumming down ⊓ on the *on beats* (the numbers) and strumming up V on the *off beats* (the &s). You're playing eighth notes! That's all there is to it.

These exercises will get you strumming eighth notes. For now, keep that foot tapping.

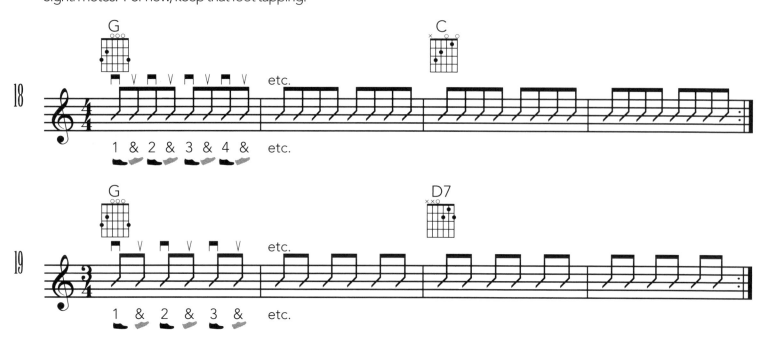

Chapter Two

LESSON 11: PUTTING IT ALL TOGETHER

It's time to use everything you've learned so far. In the following ten examples, you'll find all five of the chords you know in all kinds of rhythms. This is the preparation you need before you learn your first, full-fledged songs. Dig in!

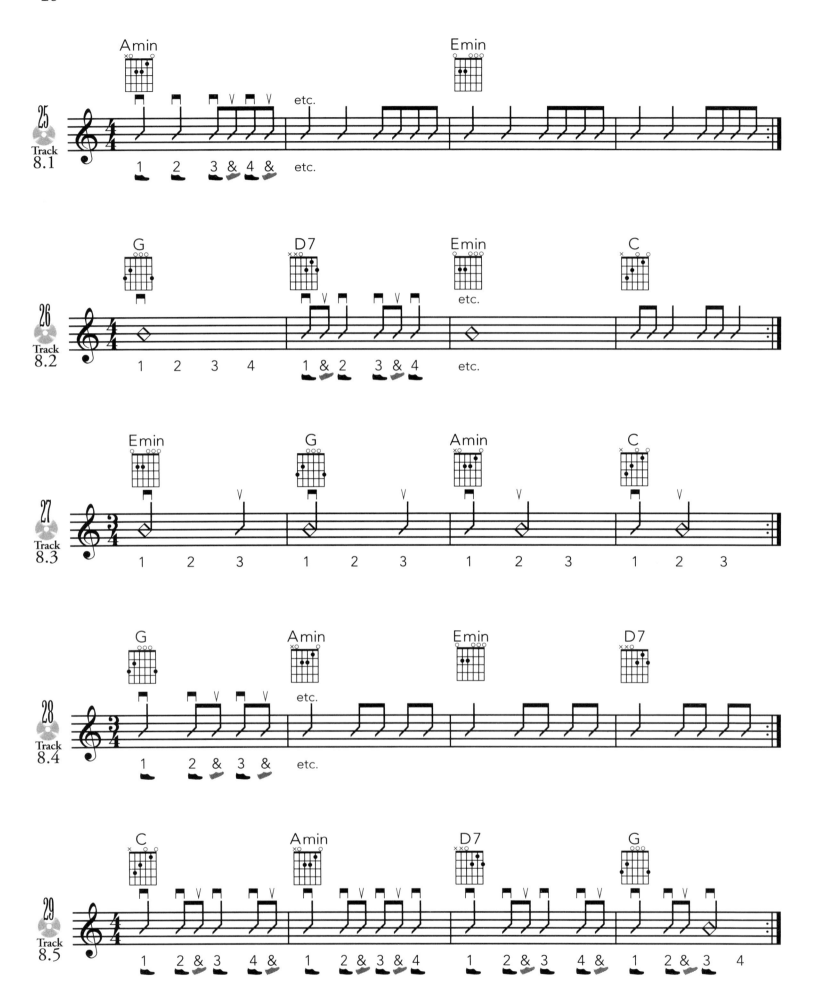

LESSON 12: YOUR FIRST FULL SONGS

This *chord progression* (a succession of chords) is in the style of the song *Stand by Me*, which was recorded by Ben E. King and written by the famous songwriting team, Lieber and Stoller. Try to lock into the beat as you strum—groove!

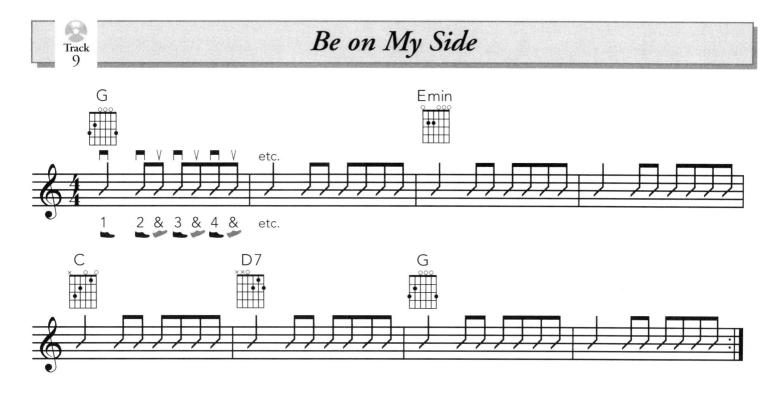

This song introduces changing chords within a measure. First, look at this example of strumming two chords in a measure. It starts with G and switches to D7 on beat 3.

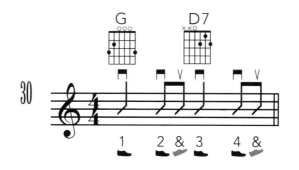

This song is in the style of Bob Dylan's *Knocking on Heaven's Door*. Practice it slowly at first and get accustomed to the quicker chord changes. Then, let it rip!

Chapter Two

LESSON 1: TABLATURE (TAB)

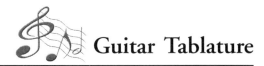

Tablature (TAB) is a graphic approach to reading music for stringed instruments. It is a simple way to communicate where the fingers should be placed on the guitar. Some types of TAB also communicate the rhythm to play. Since we will ultimately be using TAB in conjunction with standard music notation, we use a type that does not include the rhythm. This type of TAB works only if you already know the song by ear or have the standard notation available. The combination of the two—TAB and standard notation—makes an unbeatable team. Let's look at the TAB first.

Tablature is written showing six horizontal lines. Each line represents a string on the guitar.

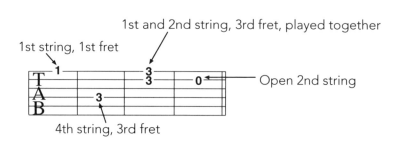

The numbers under the TAB indicate which left-hand fingers to use.

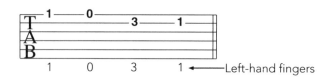

Below are some popular tunes to use for practicing your TAB reading skills.
Have fun!

Amazing Grace

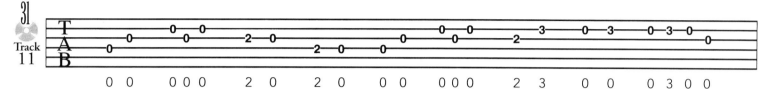

The Wedding March

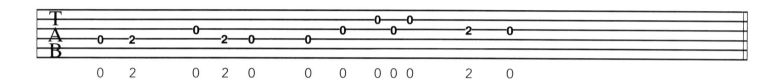

Jingle Bells

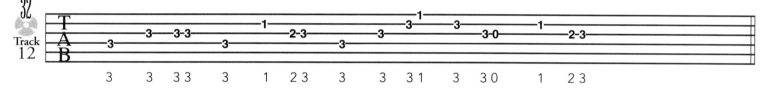

Row, Row, Row Your Boat

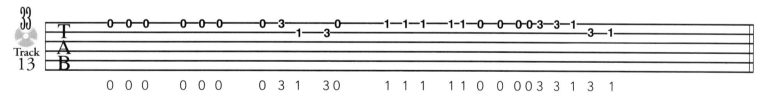

Chapter Three

LESSON 2: STANDARD MUSIC NOTATION

Standard music notation is used by all kinds of musicians from all over the world. That's what makes it so important for you to understand it. Standard music notation allows you to communicate with any other musician. Also, sooner or later you'll want to learn to play songs by your favorite artists, and the song-books you buy will assume you have this basic skill.

As you learned on page 16, guitar music is written on a staff with a treble clef (sometimes called the *G clef*). The treble clef surrounds the "G" line:

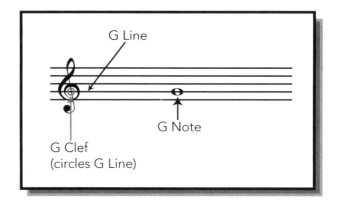

Notes are written on the lines and spaces of the staff. Each line and space has a letter name taken from the musical alphabet (A B C D E F G).

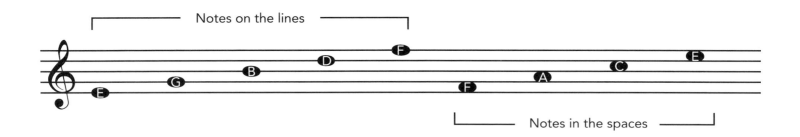

The rhythmic value of a note (how long or short it is) is indicated by its type:

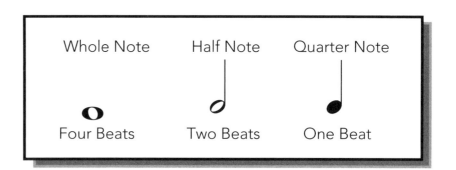

LESSON 3: NOTES ON THE 1ST STRING

The diagrams below are read just like the chord diagrams you've been reading (see page 15). Vertical lines represent strings, horizontal lines represent frets and the numbers indicate which finger to use.

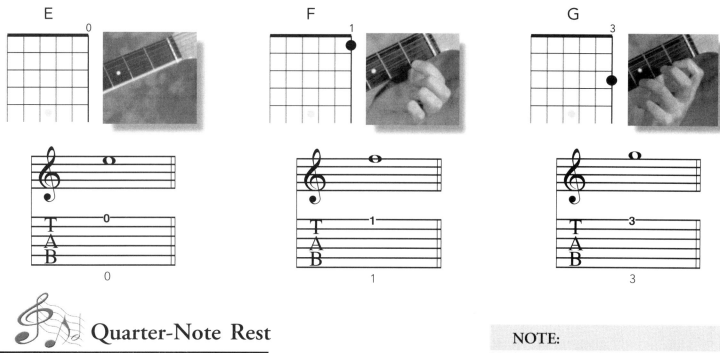

Quarter-Note Rest

The quarter rest indicates one beat of silence:

Stop any ringing string with either your left or right hand.

Practice reading the notes on the first string. Count carefully and keep a steady beat.

NOTE:

Notice that rests do not appear in the TAB. In this style of writing guitar music, almost all information pertaining to time is shown in the standard musical notation only. In the counting numbers, parentheses show where the rests fall. For example, (4) means to rest on the fourth beat.

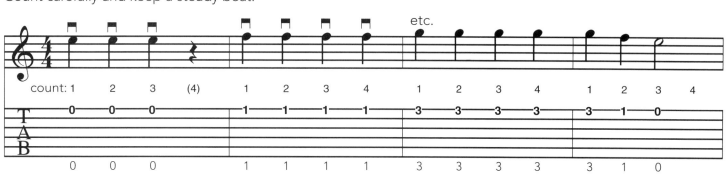

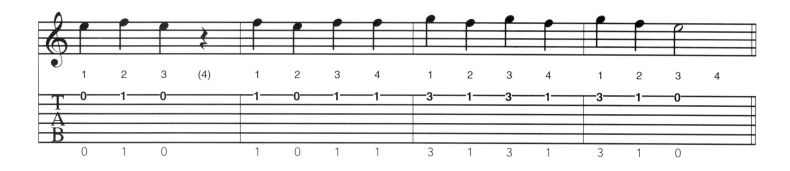

Chapter Three

LESSON 4: NOTES ON THE 2ND STRING

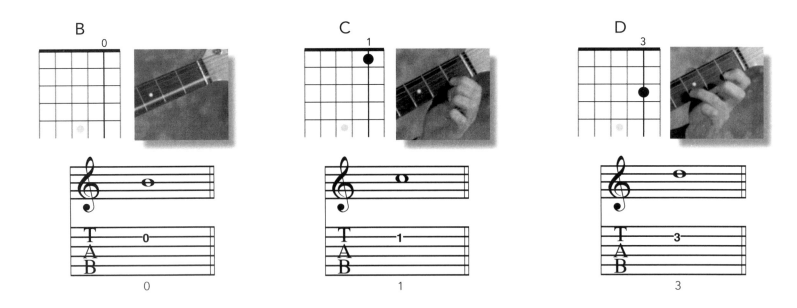

 Half-Note Rest

The half-note rest indicates two beats of silence:

Here's an exercise for reading the notes on the 2nd string. Keep counting!

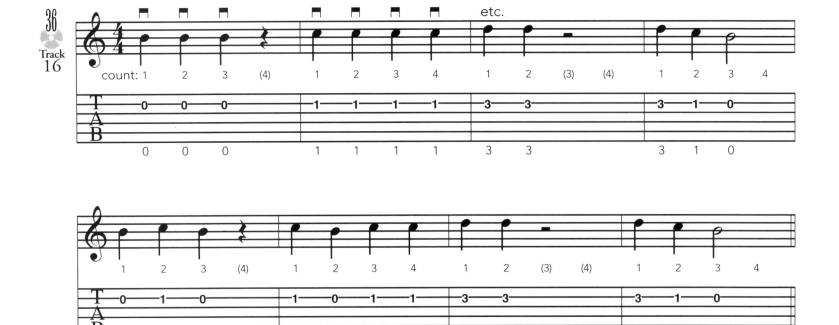

Chapter Three

LESSON 5: THE 1ST AND 2ND STRINGS COMBINED

These exercises include chord symbols along with the melodies. Your teacher or a friend can accompany you by playing the chords in a simple quarter-note strum, or you can record yourself playing the chords. If you have the CD that is available for this book, then you're in business. Playing with someone else is great practice and a lot of fun. Do it whenever possible!

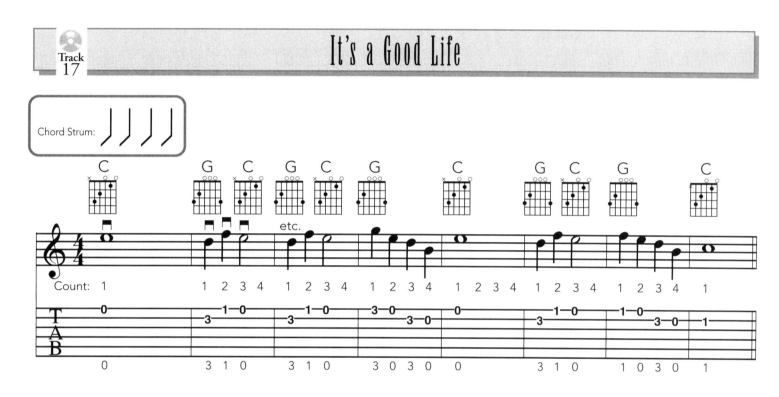

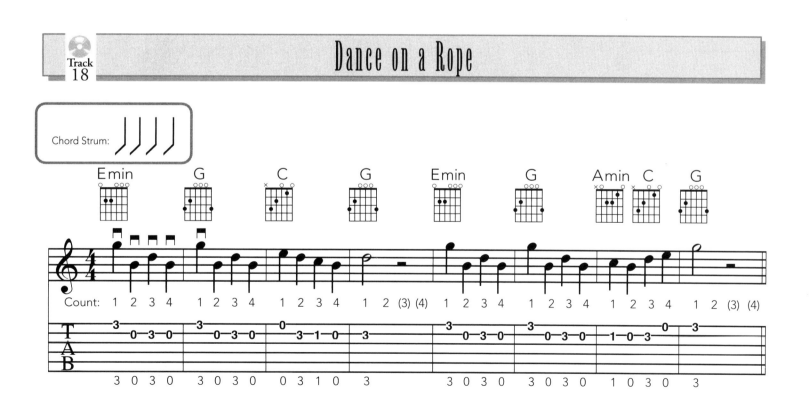

LESSON 6: NOTES ON THE 3RD STRING

 **Octaves**

You may have noticed that you have been taught two notes with the same name: G on the 1st string and G on the 3rd string. Play the two G's, one after the other. You'll hear the similarity. They are the same pitch but one is higher than the other. The closest distance between any two notes with the same name is called an *octave*, so these Gs are an octave apart.

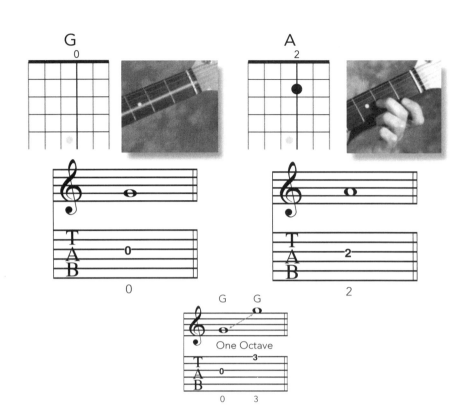

 **Whole-Note Rest**

The whole-note rest indicates four beats of silence:

Here's an exercise for practicing the notes on the 3rd string:

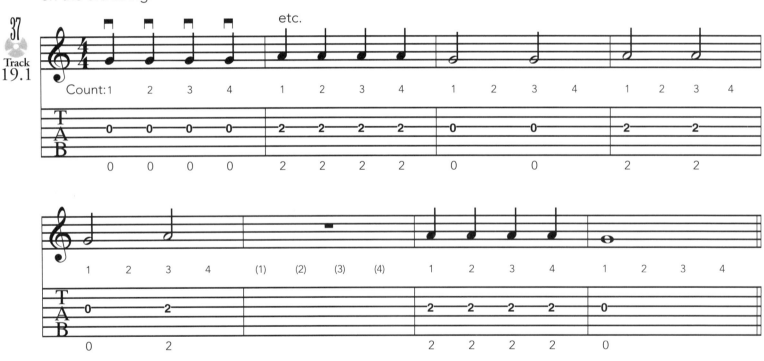

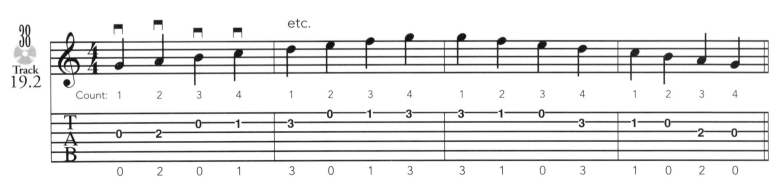

LESSON 7: NOTES ON THE 1ST, 2ND AND 3RD STRINGS

The Fermata

The *fermata* is a hold or pause sign:

A fermata sometimes occurs on the last note of a song. Hold the note for longer than its written value. Hit the last note or chord and let it fade away.

Here's a tune that uses all the notes you've learned so far. Enjoy playing it two ways: Play the melody, or strum the chords. Again, it's great fun to play with someone else. Have a friend or teacher play one part while you play the other. If you have the CD that is available for this book, spin the disc and play along.

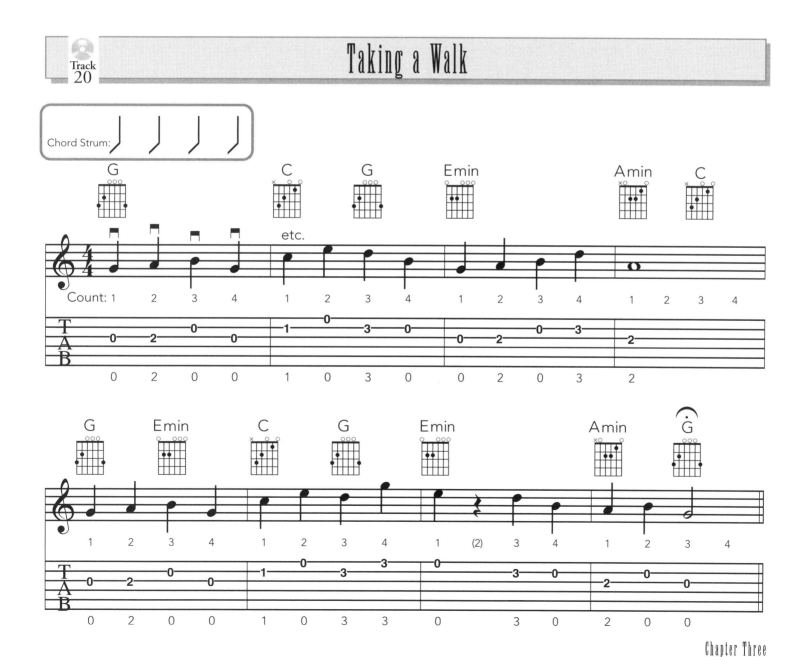

Taking a Walk

Chapter Three

LESSON 8: NOTES ON THE 4TH STRING

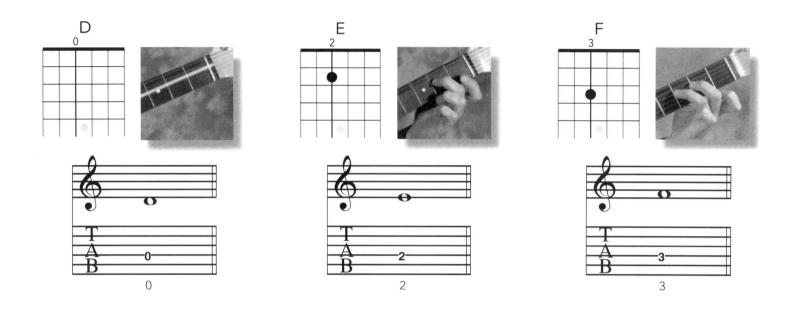

Here's an exercise for practicing the notes on the 4th string:

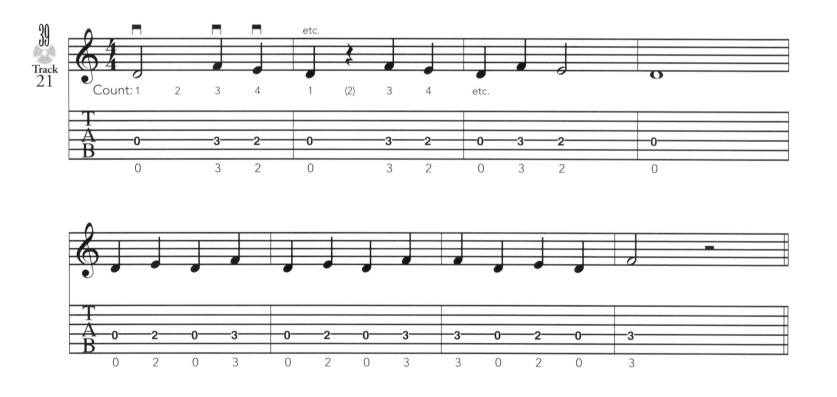

LESSON 9: NOTES ON THE 1ST, 2ND, 3RD AND 4TH STRINGS

LESSON 10: NOTES ON THE 5TH STRING

 **Ledger Lines**

Ledger lines are short horizontal lines that are used to extend the staff either higher or lower. Any note lower than D on the open 4th string will be accompanied by one or more ledger lines. The same is true for any note higher than G on the 1st string, 3rd fret.

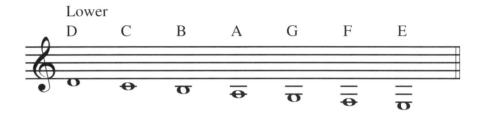

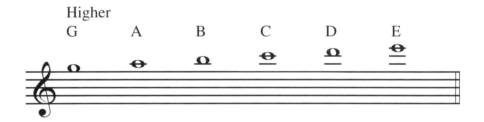

Let's look at three octaves of the musical alphabet:

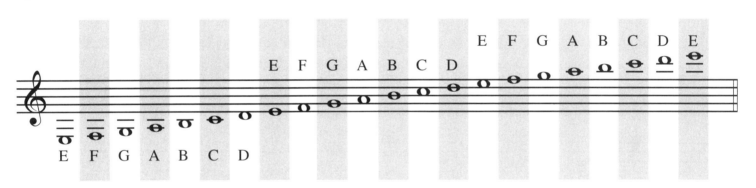

Here are your new notes:

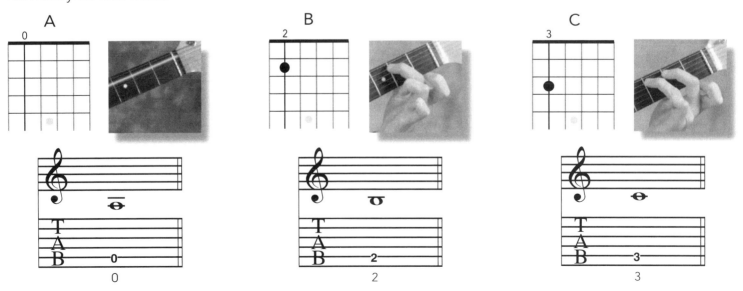

Chapter Three

Here's an exercise for the notes on the 5th string:

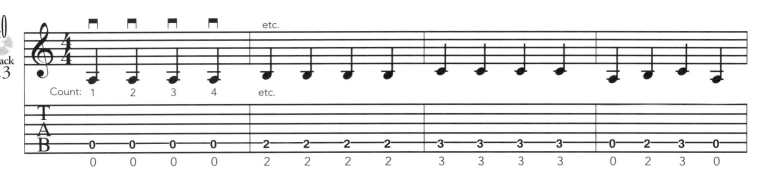

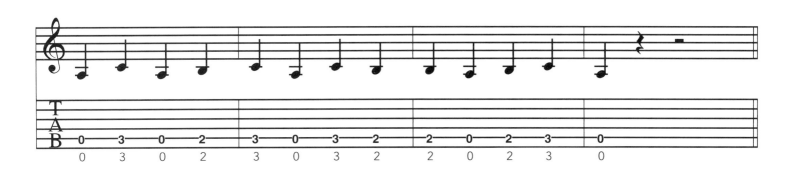

The Final Double Bar

On page 18, you learned the repeat sign:

When a song is not repeated, we use a final double barline instead. Notice that the only difference is that there are no dots:

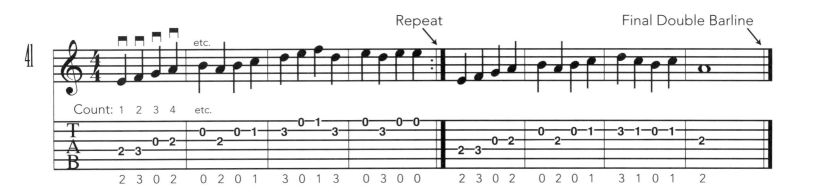

Chapter Three

LESSON 11: TIES AND ACCIDENTALS

Ties

A tie is a curved line that connects two or more notes of the same pitch. It "ties" the notes together so that the values combine to create one longer note equaling the sum of all the notes in the tie. For instance, two quarter notes (each equaling one beat) tied together equal two beats. Do not strike the second note in a tie.

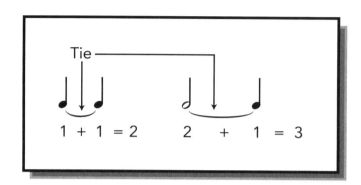

Accidentals

Accidentals are signs that raise, lower or return a note to its original pitch. The sharp sign ♯ raises a note one fret. The distance of one fret is called a *half step*. The flat sign ♭ lowers a note one fret.

The Sharp

The Flat
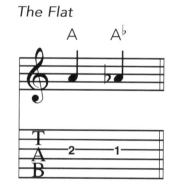

The natural sign ♮ returns a note that has been sharped or flatted to its original pitch.

The Natural

An accidental remains in force for the rest of the measure. For example, if a note is sharped, it stays sharp for the duration of the measure unless marked with a natural sign.

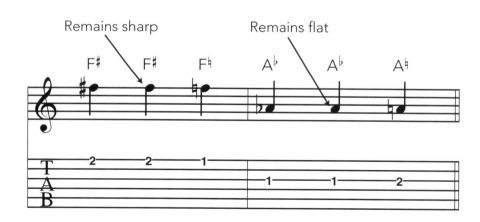

Chapter Three

Here's a tune that uses accidentals and ties. Have fun!

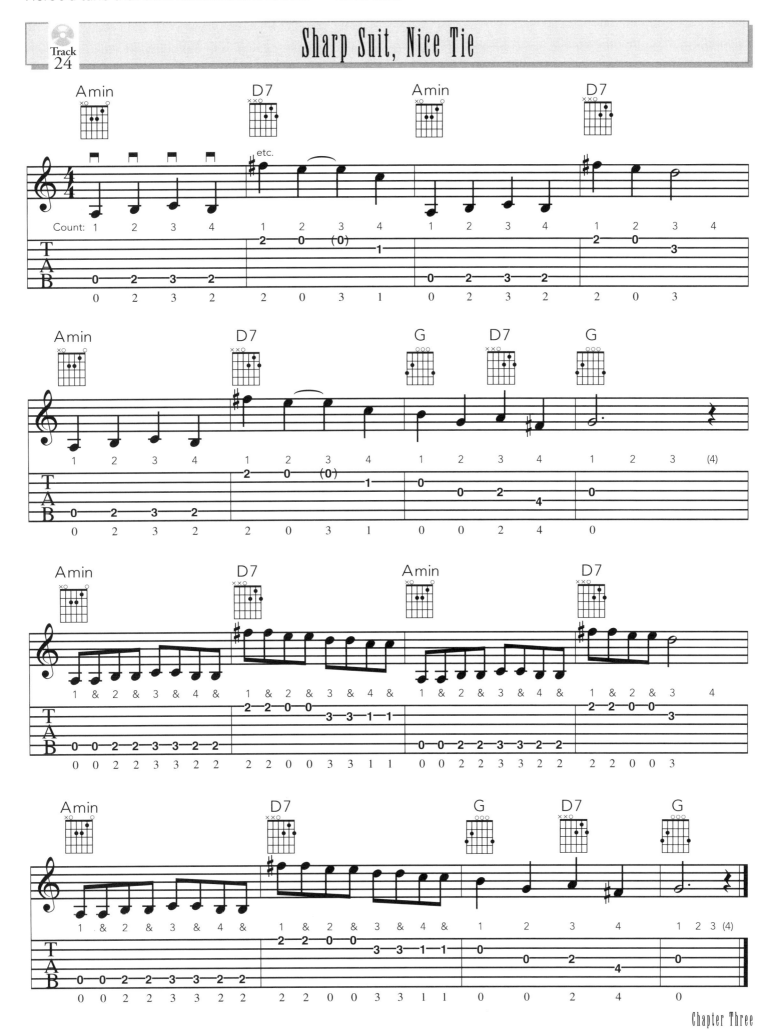

LESSON 12: NOTES ON THE 6TH STRING

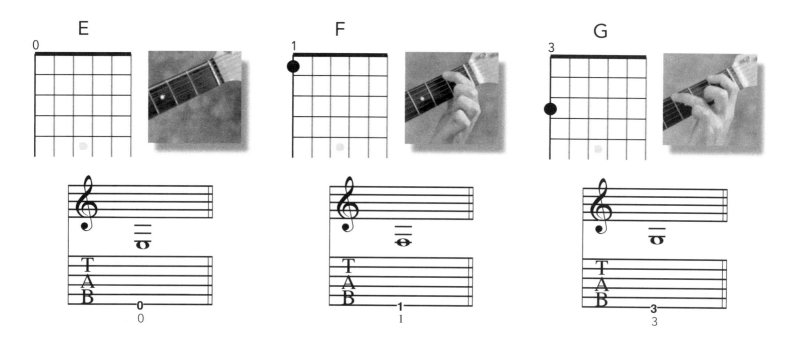

While there are lots of ledger lines here (see page 38), counting them isn't the trick to learning these low notes. Learn to recognize them. They look a lot different from one another. Don't sweat counting lines. Save it for tax time. Guitar is fun. Taxes aren't.

Here's a Tip...

Any accidental (sharp or flat) can be called by either a sharp name or a flat name. For example, F♯ can also be called G♭ because they fall on the same fret. They sound the same but have different names. Notes that are related in this way are said to be *enharmonic equivalents*. Often, sharps will be used for ascending melodies and flats for descending melodies, which is the case in example 42.

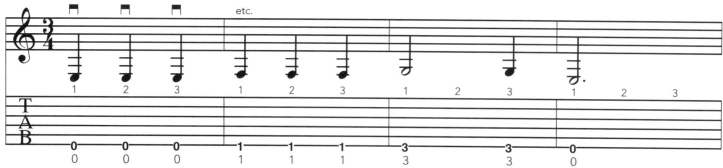

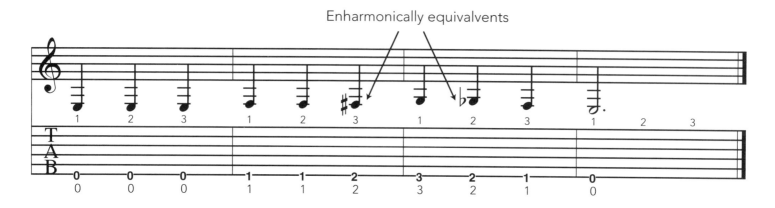

Enharmonically equivalvents

Chapter Three

LESSON 13: CHORDS WRITTEN IN TAB AND STANDARD MUSIC NOTATION

Sometimes we see notes stacked on top of each other. This means that they are played simultaneously and represent a chord. Here are all the chords you have learned so far written this way:

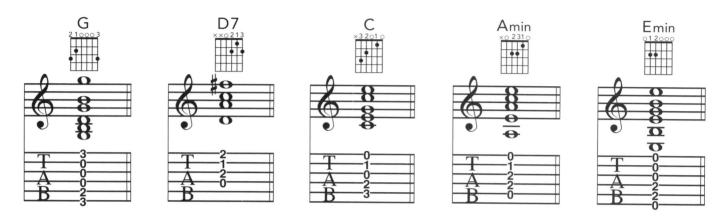

While you won't find a lot of this notational style in this book, you will as you progress to more advanced levels. Example 43 will give you a little experience with it. The chord symbols above the music and the TAB below will make the reading easy.

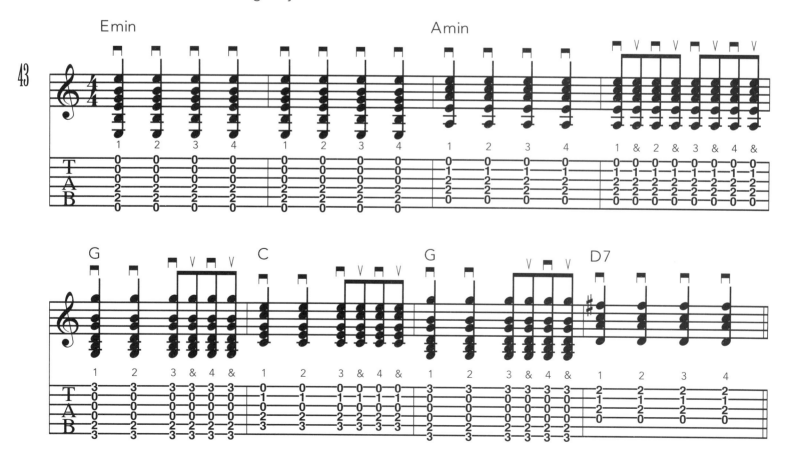

Chapter Four

LESSON 1: NEW CHORDS: A, D AND E

These are some of the most commonly used guitar chords. Folks with big fingers may want to rearrange the fingerings for the A chord to 2-1-3 instead of 1-2-3. If you have trouble squeezing your sausage-like appendages into one fret, try laying one finger across the 2nd fret (this is called a *barre* chord, see pages 52 and 92).

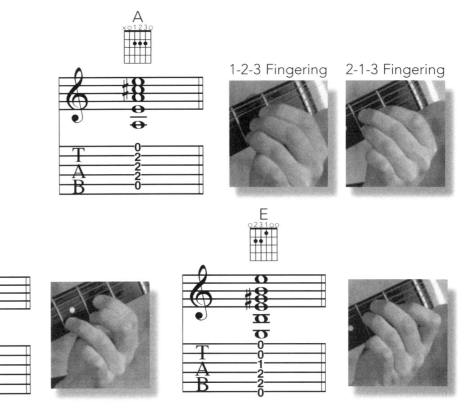

Example 44 will give these new chords a workout. It's a good idea to practice each individual chord change very slowly before trying to strum through the whole example.

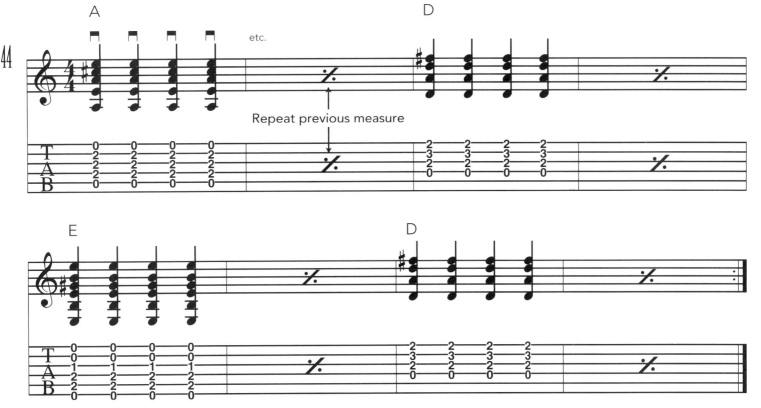

LESSON 2: EIGHTH-NOTE RESTS

Eighth-note rests have the same value as eighth notes—half a beat (see page 24). The rest falls on either the first half of the beat (the *on* beat) or on the second half (the *off* beat). As with quarter and half rests, the eighth rest indicates silence. Use your right or left hand to stop the strings from ringing.

> Remember, rests do not appear in TAB. Make sure you are always reading the music and TAB, *not just the TAB*.

The next two examples start with a measure of straight eighth notes. The rests appear in the second measure.

Rest on the *off* beats:

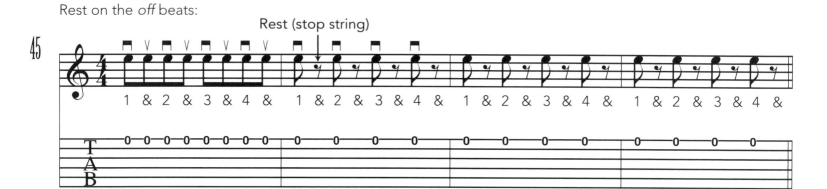

Rest on the *on* beats:

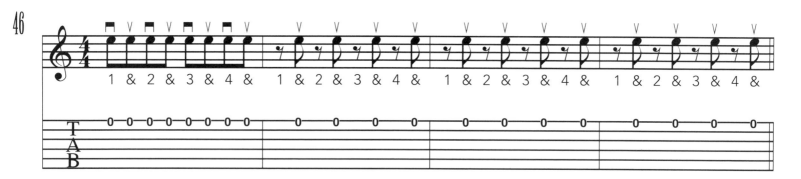

Examples 47 and 48 show eighth note rests as they appear when writing chords in standard notation:

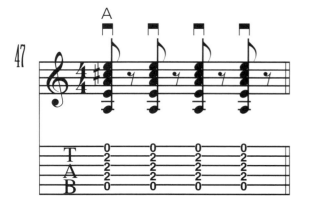
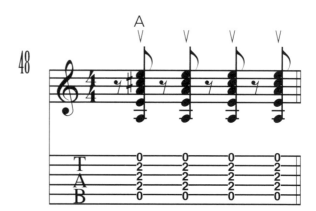

Chapter Four

The following examples show the eighth-note rest in strum notation:

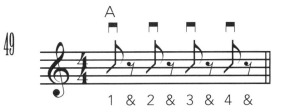

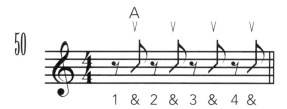

Examples 51 through 54 demonstrate the variety eighth-note rests can bring to strumming rhythms. Enjoy.

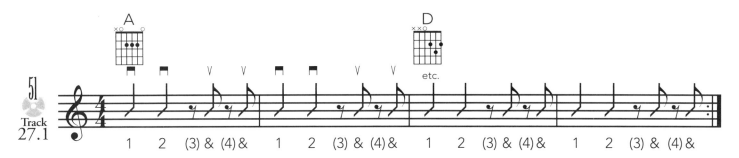

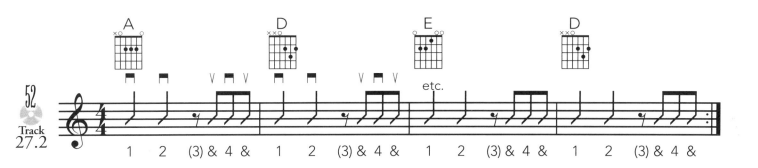

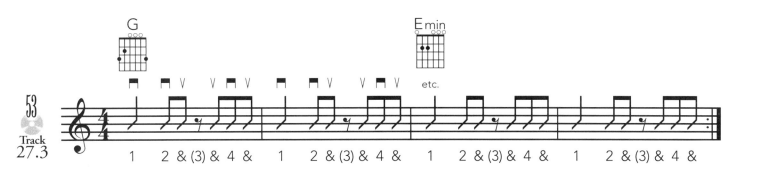

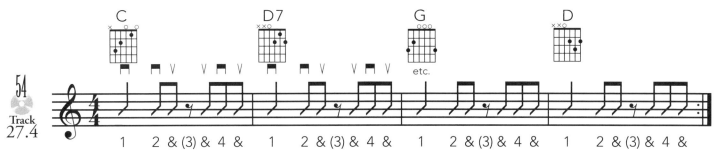

Careful, now—this isn't kid stuff! Practice counting and playing the rhythms to this tune, in the style of Jimmy Buffet's *Margaritaville*. We recommend that you put off pouring the margaritas until after practice, though.

Pay close attention to the ties!

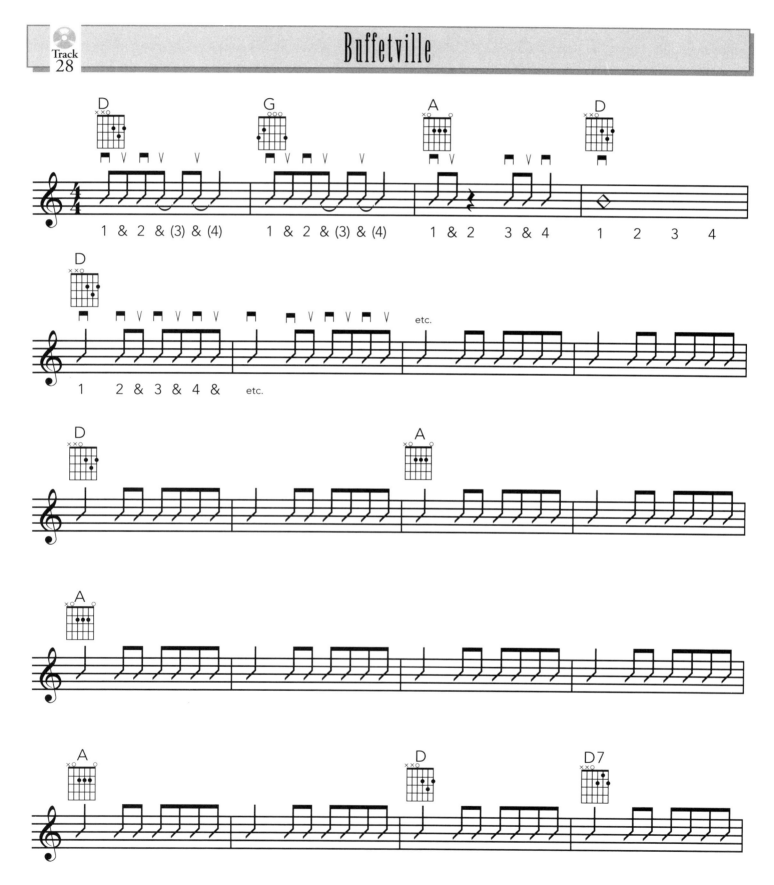

Chapter Four

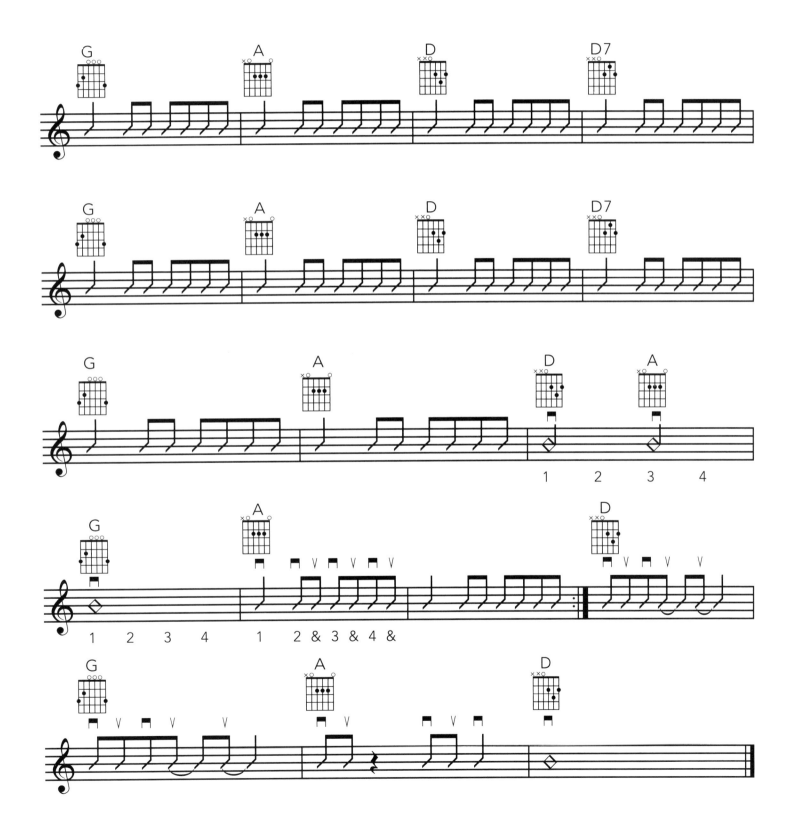

Wild Thing was performed masterfully by Jimi Hendrix. But if you're old enough to remember the original version by The Troggs, this book is definitely for you! Enjoy strumming through *Crazy Girl*, in the style of that classic tune. Notice that it's the eighth-note rest that puts the "wild" in the rhythm. Stop the strings with your right hand for that half beat and it will really rock.

Chapter Four

LESSON 3: REGGAE ACCOMPANIMENT RHYTHM

Sometimes a *rhythm simile* is shown at the beginning of a song. This tells the person playing the chords what rhythm to play. This rhythm simile should be strummed throughout the song. Example 55 is the rhythm simile for the next tune. The reggae style is defined by this off-beat rhythm with eighth-note rests and up strokes.

Reggae Tune is in the style of the Bob Marley song, *Stir It Up.* You should learn to play both the tune and strum the chords in the rhythm provided in example 55.

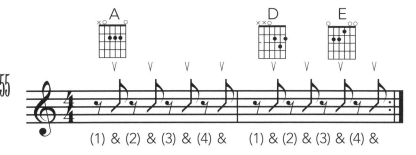

* Still sharp!

LESSON 4: NEW CHORDS: F AND G7

The F Chord Barre

The F chord involves a new technique called a *barre*. A barre occurs when two or more notes are played with the same finger. To play the F chord, lay the end segment of your 1st finger across the 1st and 2nd strings at the 1st fret. Many players find it helpful to bring in the left elbow closer to the body. This provides a little extra leverage. Despair not! This is hard for everyone, at first. Practice this for just a few minutes at a time until it gets easy.

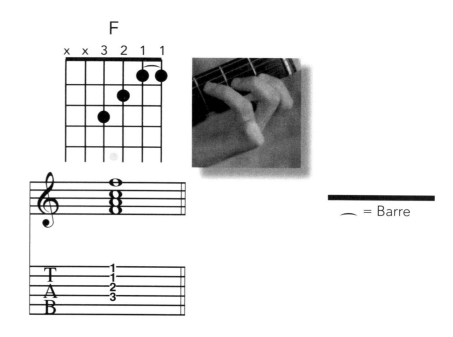

Below is a song in the style of The Rolling Stones' song, *You Can't Always Get What You Want*. This is a great song for trying the F chord.

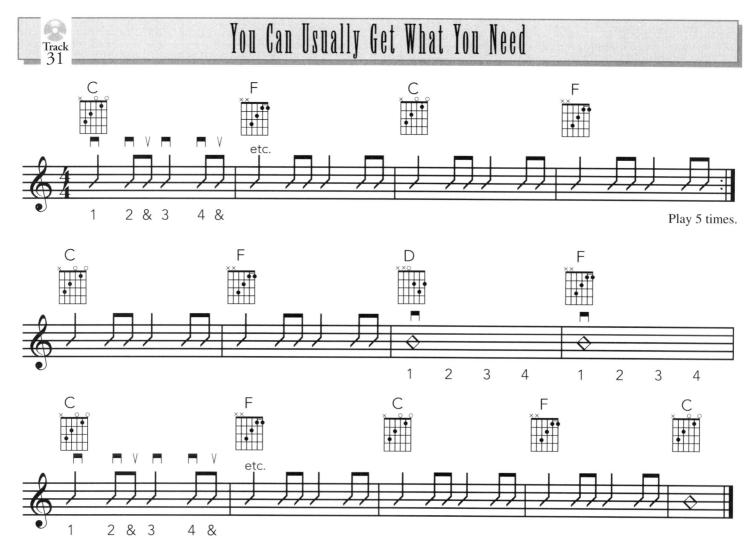

Chapter Four

Ron Zuskin, 51
Clinical Social Worker

Ron is the Director of Training at the University of Maryland School of Social Work. He has played guitar for 35 years. He decided to stop buying better guitars and get better at playing instead.

The G7 Chord

This chord is a breeze to play and works great when paired with a C chord.

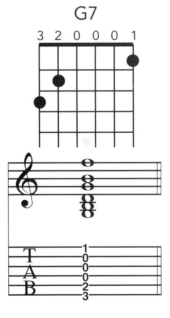

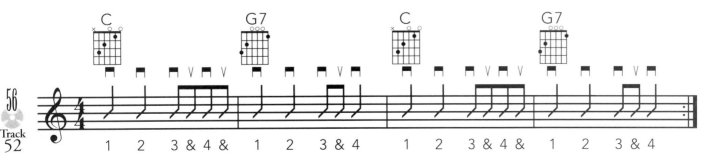

Track 52

Chapter Four

LESSON 5: MUSICAL ROAD MAPS

Songs often have parts that repeat. Musicians have developed methods that make it easier to condense written music so that these repetitions don't take lots of space on the page. This system of signs and symbols that leads us from place to place on the page can be thought of as comprising a musical "road map."

Below is demonstration of how this works. On the right is a step-by-step explanation:

Step 1. Start the song at the first measure. Play the first four measures. At the fourth measure, you will notice the number 1 with a bracket. There is a repeat sign at the end of the measure. This is a *first ending*. Go back to the beginning of the song and start again.

Step 2. Play from the beginning of the song until you reach the first ending. Skip over the first ending and go directly to the *second ending*. Play from that point on until you see *D.C. al Coda* (Da Capo al Coda). This means go back to the beginning and play until you see the first *Coda* sign ⊕. A Coda is an ending section of a piece.

Step 3. Skip over all the music between the first Coda sign and the second. The second Coda sign is always near the end of the written music. Play from the second Coda sign to the end.

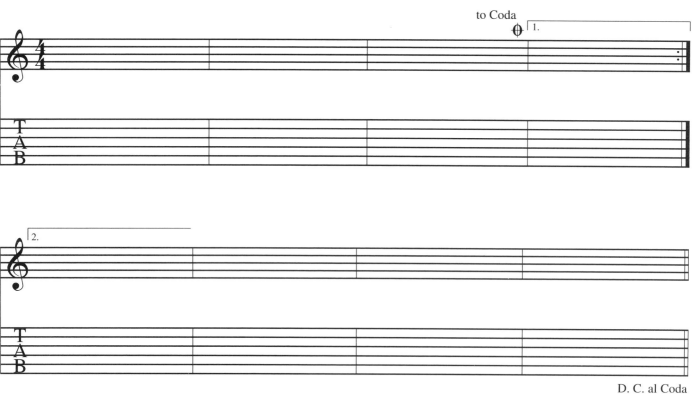

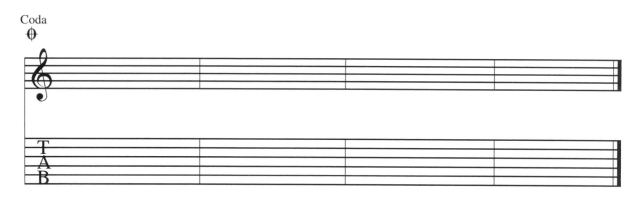

Twist and Shout, by Burt Berns and Phil Medley, was the Isley Brothers' first hit and was later given new life by The Beatles. *Twisted*, in the style of this great rock'n'roll tune, makes good use of both new chords, F and G7. Try not to think about how we looked doing this dance and enjoy strumming the chords.

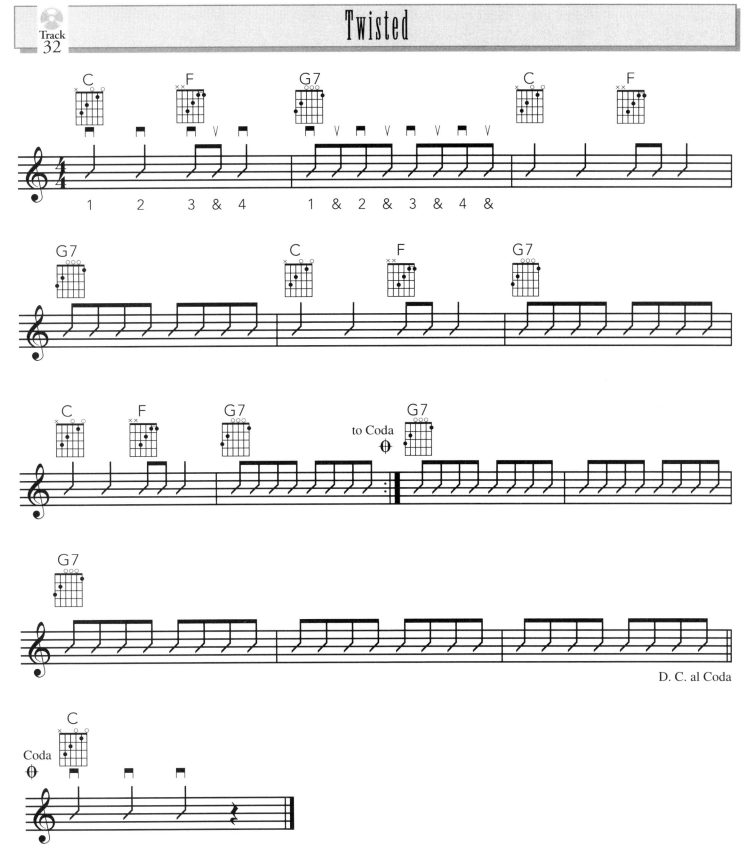

Chapter Five

LESSON 1: FLATPICKING ARPEGGIOS

Flatpicking is a term used to describe single-line, pick-style guitar playing. We have been using the pick to strum chords. Now we are going to break those chords apart and play the notes separately. When a chord is broken, with the notes played one after the other, it is called an *arpeggio*.

Example 57 shows an arpeggio for each chord you have learned so far. Practice each one until mastered. You may have to watch your right hand closely, since your pick will have to skip strings often. Try to get a feel for the distance between the strings so that, eventually, you can find any string without looking.

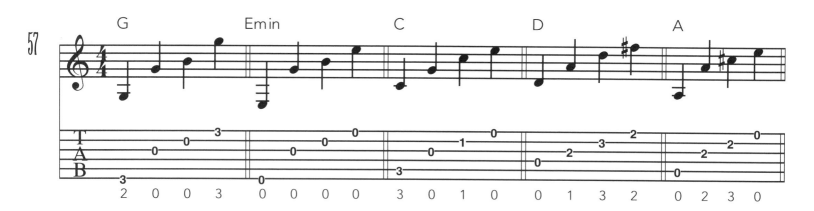

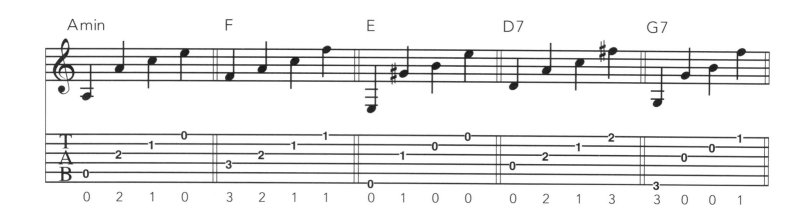

Dark, Cloudy Day will give you some additional practice flatpicking arpeggios.

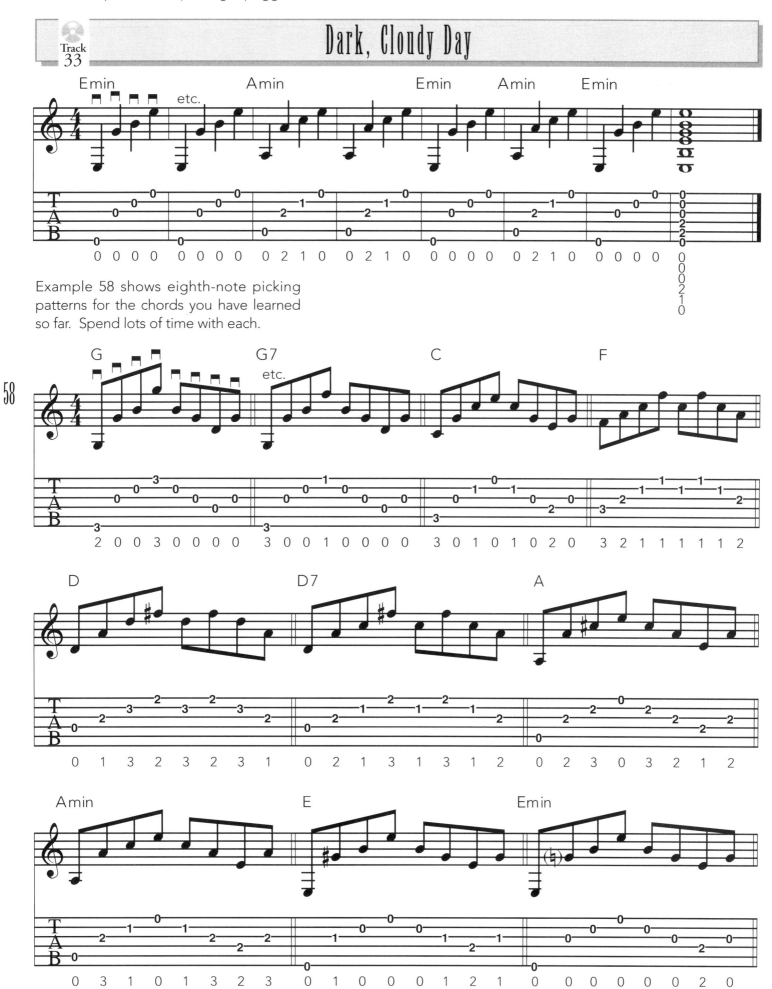

Example 58 shows eighth-note picking patterns for the chords you have learned so far. Spend lots of time with each.

This song is in the style of Eric Clapton's *Wonderful Tonight*.

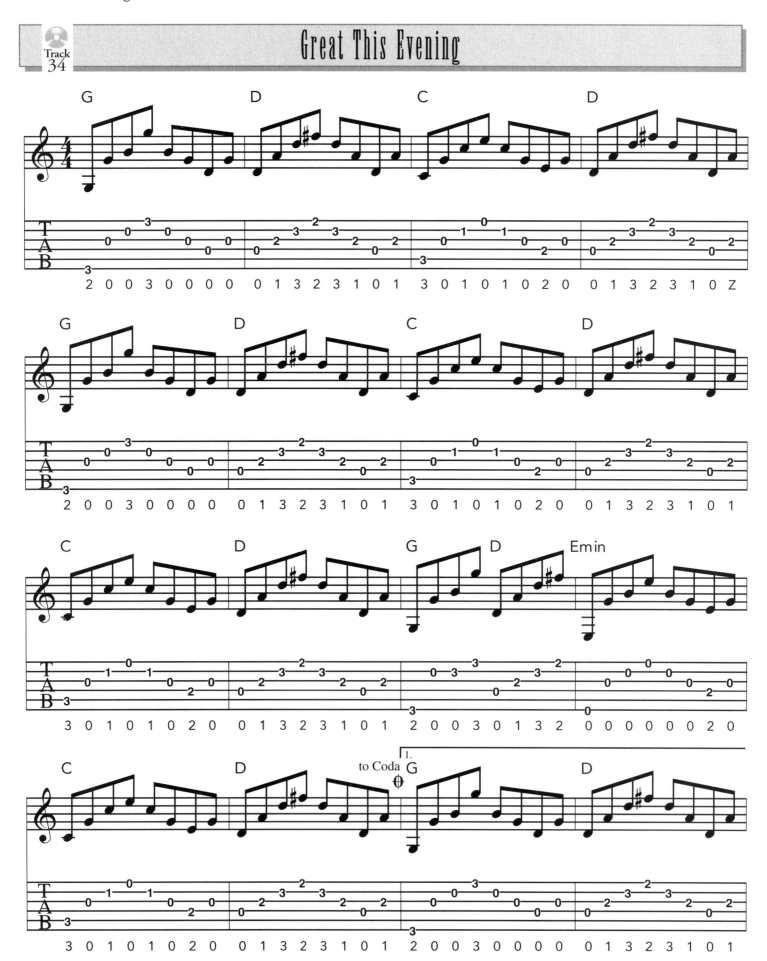

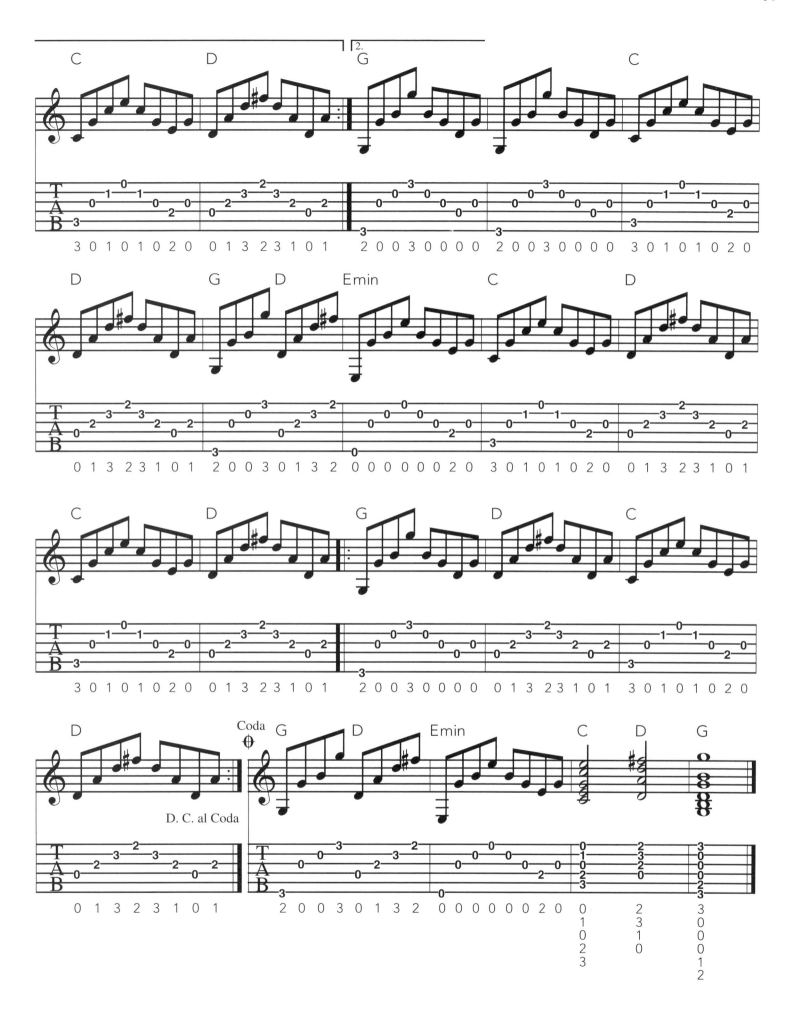

LESSON 2: BASS-STRUM TECHNIQUE

The bass-strum technique adds another dimension to flatpicking. Instead of arpeggiating the chord, we split the chord into two parts:

1) the *bass note*, which is the lowest pitch in the chord; and
2) the remainder of the notes in the chord.

Below are examples of each chord we have learned so far in the bass-strum format:

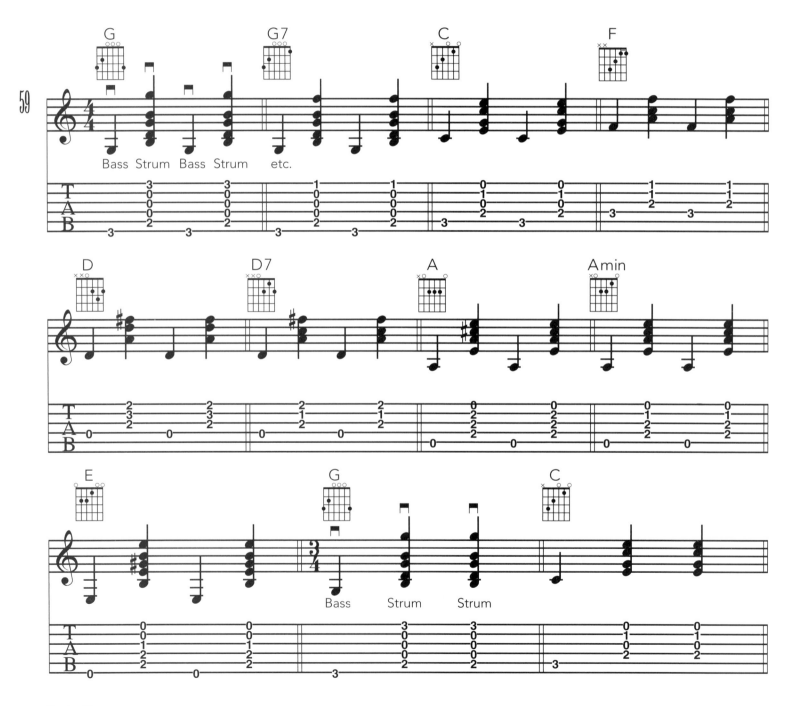

The bass-strum technique is a common accompaniment style in country music and in other country-influenced styles. Here's a country tune for practicing your pickin' and grinin'.

LESSON 3: SLASH CHORDS AND MUTING

Slash Chords

So far, the chords we have been playing have had the *root* as the bass note. The root is the fundamental note of a chord that gives the chord its name. For example, the root of a C chord is C. *Slash chords* are chord symbols that indicate something other than the root is in the bass position. The letter to the left of the slash (/) represents the chord to be played. The letter to the right of the slash is the note in the bass position.

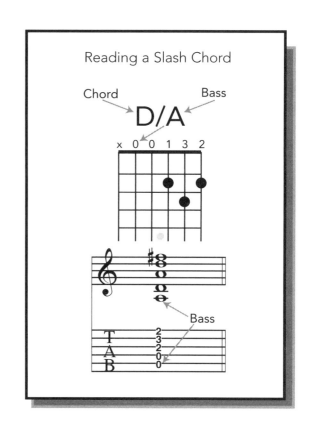

Muting

The second slash chord in example 60 has an "x" over the 5th string. This means that the 5th string should be muted. To mute a string is to silence it somehow. In this case, mute the 5th string by letting the side of the 1st finger, which is playing a note on the 6th string, lightly touch the 5th. This will keep the 5th string from vibrating.

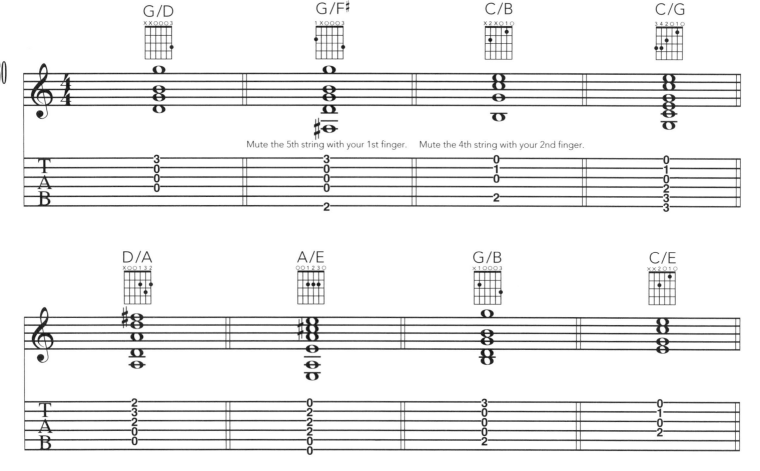

Chapter Five

Many of our favorite classic tunes use slash chords. This tune is in the style *Rocky Racoon* by the Beatles. Study the chords in the first ending. Going from C to C/B, then back to Amin at the beginning of the song, creates a nice bass line—C, B, A. It brings us around to the top of the tune very smoothly. Slash chords are often used for this very reason.

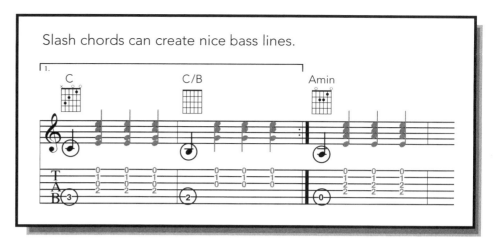

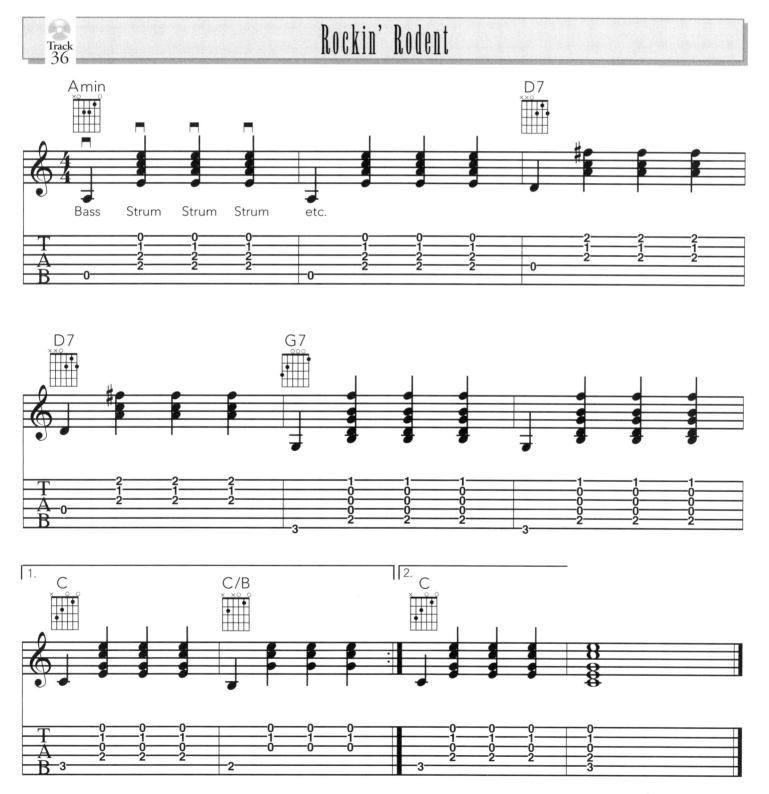

LESSON 4: ROOT-5TH STRUM TECHNIQUE

On page 62, you learned that the root of a chord is the note that gives the chord its name. Count up five notes from the root and you have the 5th. The 5th of a C chord is G (C-1, D-2, E-3, F-4, G-5).

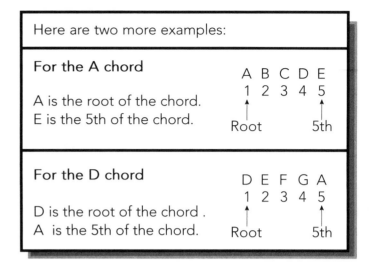

Example 61 shows the root-5th strum technique applied to all the chords you have learned so far.

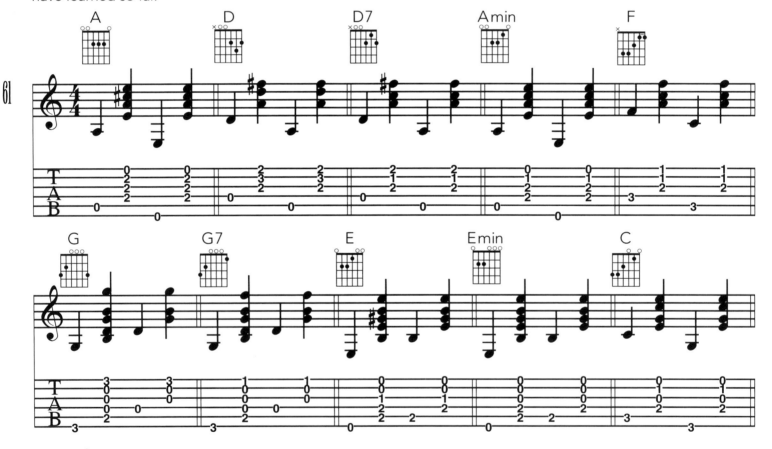

Try it in 3/4.

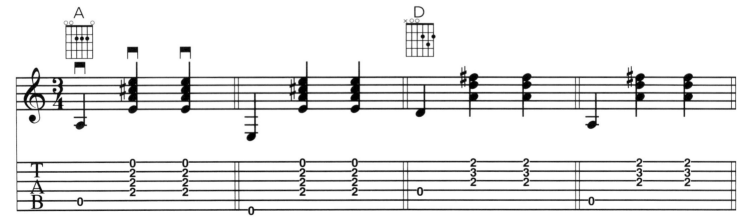

Chapter Five

You learned about rhythmic similes on page 51. Here's a waltz-time simile using the root-5th technique for *Waltzing My Baby*.

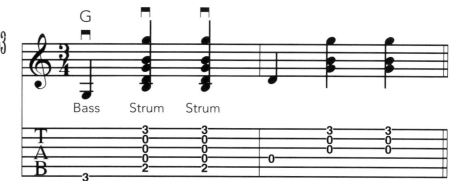

Learn to play the chords for *Waltzing My Baby* using the rhythmic simile in example 63, and learn to play the melody too. Either play along with the CD available for this book or record yourself playing one of the parts. Have fun!

DOTTED NOTES

A dot to the right of a note indicates the note's value is increased by half. A dotted half note equals three beats. A dotted quarter note equals one and a half beats.

Chapter Five

The root-5th strum technique works great for this song in the style of Jimmy Buffet's *Let's Get Drunk*.

Let's Party

Track 38

Chapter Five

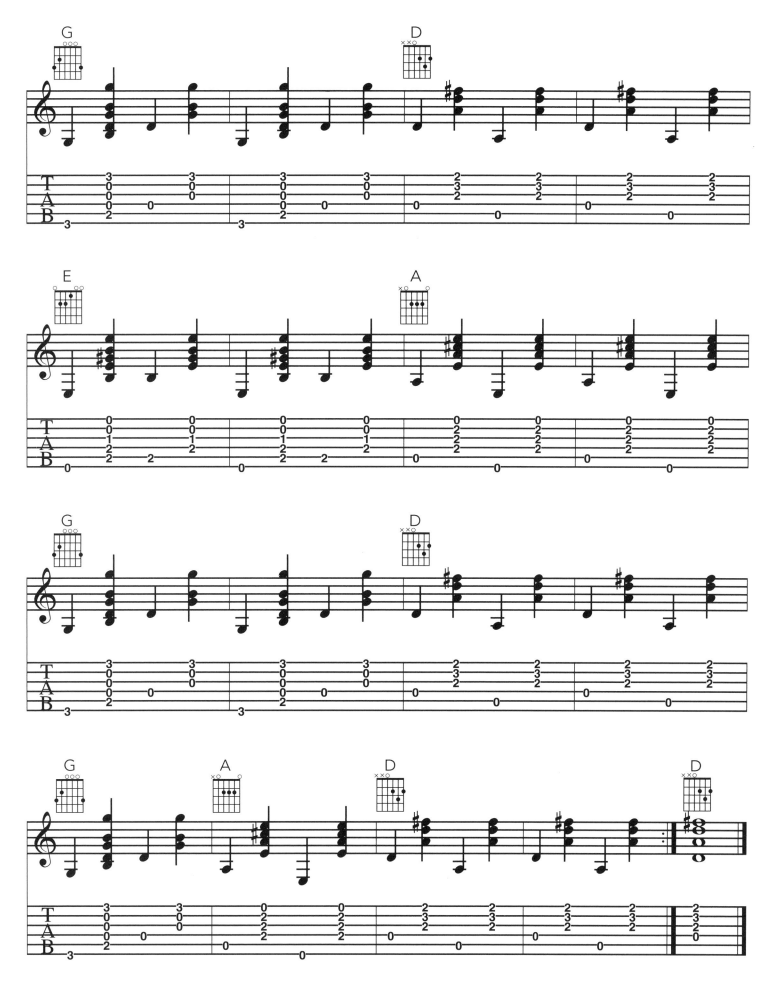

Chapter Six

LESSON 1: FINGERSTYLE—THUMB VS. FINGERS

Fingerstyle is similar to flatpicking in that we arpeggiate chords. The difference is we will be using the fingers of the right hand individually. This is an important technique for guitarists who love folk music and the work of singer/songwriters such as James Taylor and Joni Mitchell. So, put down the pick and let's go.

The fingers of the right hand are as follows:

Thumb .... *p*
Index .... *i*
Middle .... *m*
Ring .... *a*

Examples 64 through 66 show various ways to play fingerstyle on a G chord.

Try to keep your right hand from bouncing. Make full movements with the right-hand fingers and let them follow through towards the palm of the hand. It's the same principle at work here as in a golf stroke or tennis swing.

Some people grow their fingernails long and use those to help create a big sound (most notably, classical guitarists). Some folks prefer fingerpicks. It's up to you. just be careful not to play too softly.

Example 66 shows a few options for fingerstyle playing in 3/4.

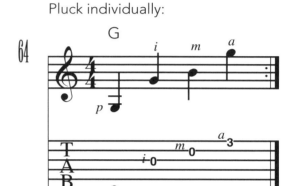

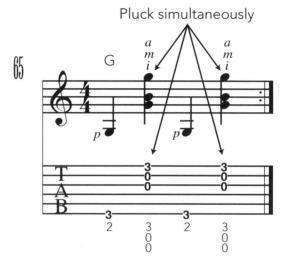

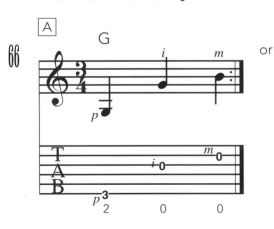

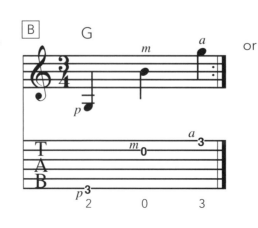

There is an endless number of fingerstyle patterns available to us, especially when you put eighth notes into the equation. Try example 67 for a taste of eighth-note fingerstyle playing.

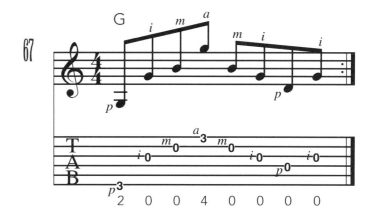

Here is a tune to play with fingerstyle technique:

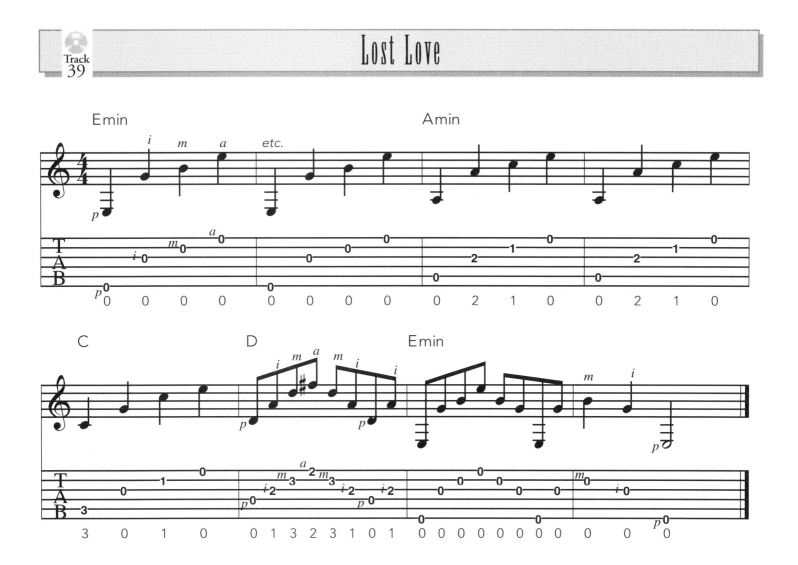

LESSON 2: FINGERSTYLE—THUMB AND FINGERS

Sometimes two notes can be played simultaneously, even if the rest of the chord is arpeggiated. Try to keep *i* and *m* poised to play while *a* and *p* strike the strings.

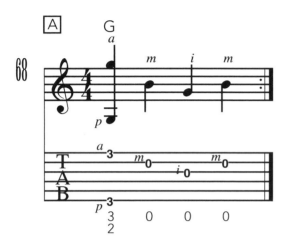

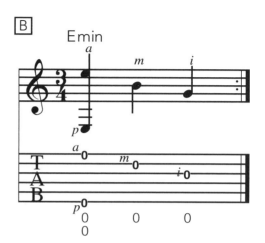

Here's a tune to play that uses this technique:

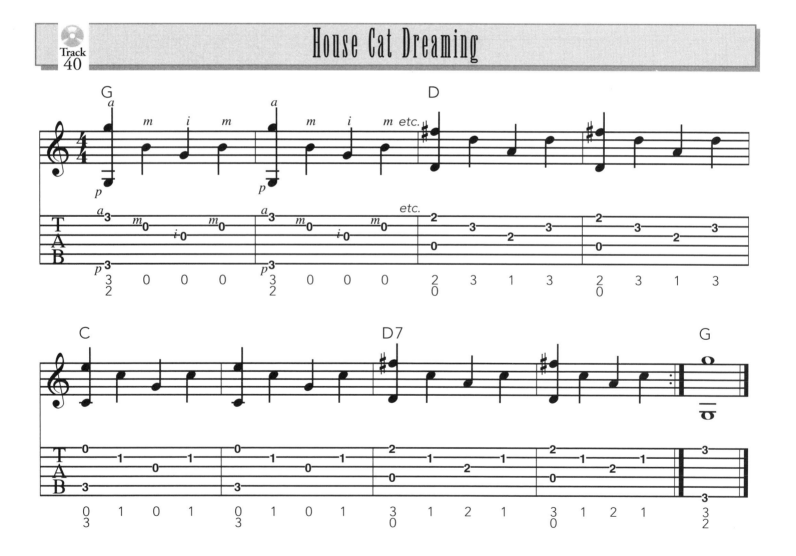

Chapter Six

LESSON 3: FINGERSTYLE ROOTS AND 5THS

Let's try adapting the root-5th technique you learned on page 64 to fingerstyle. Use the thumb (*p*) for the roots and 5ths. This can be applied to all the chords you have learned so far.

Below are examples of root-5th fingerstyle using the G chord:

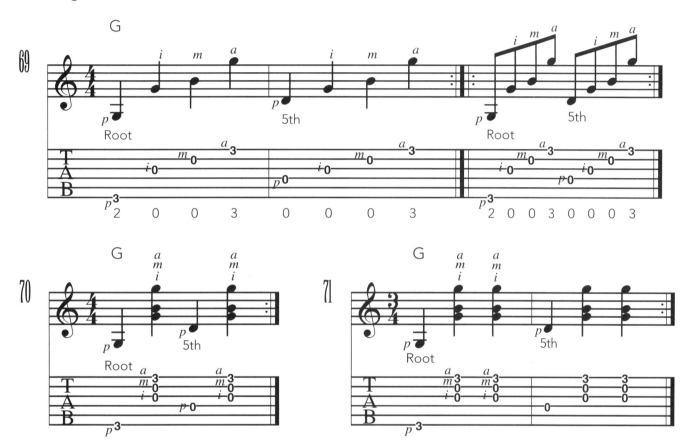

Lawrenence enjoys Bob Dylan, Neil Young and the The Beatles. His musical goal is to have fun jamming with other musicians.

LESSON 4: LIFE BEYOND THE 3RD FRET

As you know, ledger lines are used to show notes that are higher or lower than the five lines and four spaces provided on the staff (see page 38). The time has come to move to higher ground—past the high G (3rd fret, 1st string).

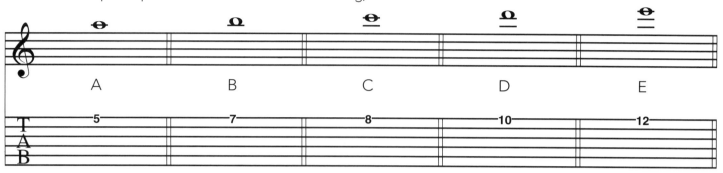

The melody in *the Rain in Spain* is played by the *a* finger on the 1st string. Play these notes a little louder than the others.

Chapter Six

Neal has enjoyed music his entire life. His favorite artists are Phish, The Greatful Dead and The Beatles.

Neal Shapiro, 34
Scrap Metal Recycler

LESSON 1: NEW CHORDS—A7 AND E7

These 7 chords are easy to remember because they are both made by simply removing one finger from a familiar major chord. Compare the chords on page 45 to these and you'll get the idea.

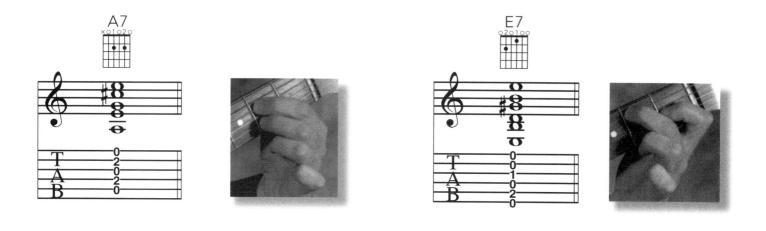

Example 72 is a simple warm-up for these chords.

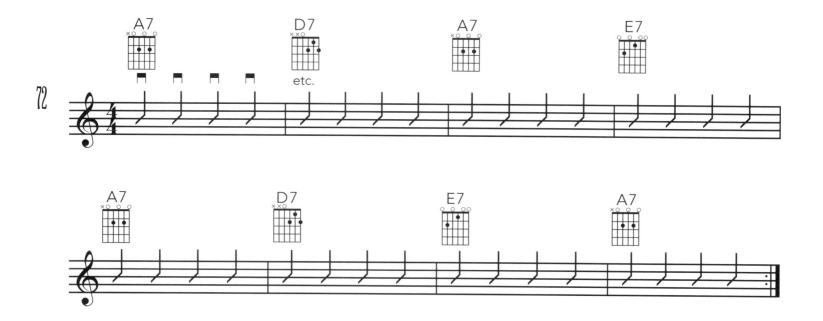

LESSON 2: NEW CHORD—C7

Here is your first four-finger chord. You will find it very familiar—just add your pinky to the C chord you learned all the way back on page 22, and you're there!

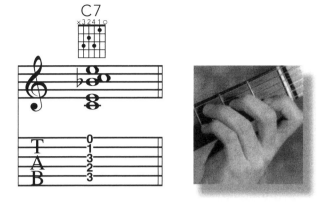

Try strumming through example 73.

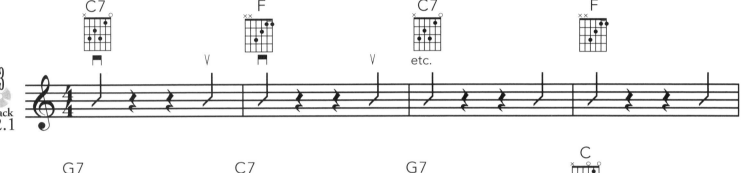

Since example 74 is fingerstyle, you can leave your 2nd finger out of the C7 chord.

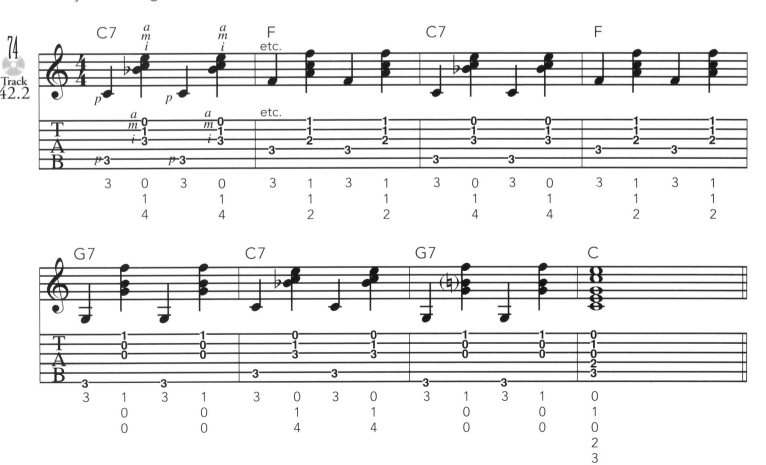

LESSON 1: THE BLUES

The blues is one of the few true American art forms. The traditional blues takes its shape in what is called a *twelve-bar blues* (*bar* is another word for measure). This is a twelve measure pattern of chords that has become so common that every musician in the Western world knows it.

A pattern of chord changes is called a *progression*. The most common chord progression for in a twelve-bar blues uses just three chords that are numbered with Roman numerals: I (1), IV (4) and V (5). We find these chords the same way we found the 5th in the root-5th strumming technique on page 64—by counting

To play a blues in the key of A, follow the musical alphabet starting with A.

A	B	C	D	E	F	G
1	2	3	4	5	6	7
			IV	V		

In A, the I, IV and V chords are A, D and E, respectively.

If we want to play a blues in the key of D:

D	E	F	G	A	B	C
1	2	3	4	5	6	7
I			IV	V		

In D, the I, IV and V chords are D, G and A, respectively.

The example below shows how these three chords—I, IV and V—are used in a twelve-bar blues progression. Just plug in the chords of the key you would like to use.

 The Twelve-Bar Blues Progression

Here's a Tip...

Sometimes a IV chord is used in the second measure. Return to the I chord in the third measure and proceed as written. This is shown in parentheses in the example below. This technique is called a "quick four."

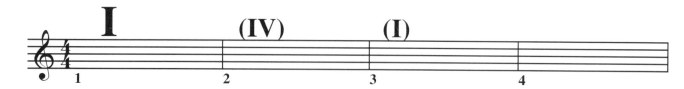

LESSON 2: PLAYIN' THE BLUES

As you play through this blues in A, you will recognize this common chord progression.

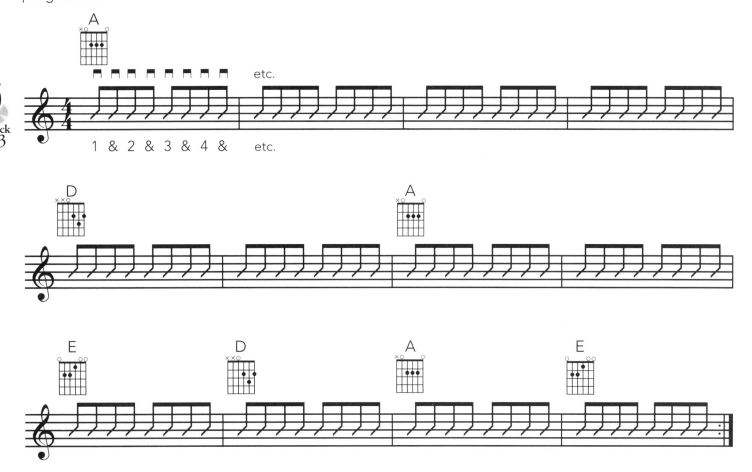

Here's a Tip...

Play your blues tune as many times as you like. To bring it to a rousing, final-sounding close, strum the I chord (in this case, A).

"My job is sometimes very stressful. Playing guitar helps relieve the stress. This is something I look forward to at the end of my day. It exercises the right side of my brain."

Anne Slein, 41
Human Resources Manager

LESSON 3: EIGHTH-NOTE TRIPLETS

The blues is just as much a *feel* as it is a chord progression. One of the most common aspects of the blues feel is the *eighth-note triplet*. An eighth-note triplet is three eighth notes played in the time of two. Say "Tri-pa-let" while tapping your foot. Every time your foot hits the floor, start the first syllable. That's the triplet feel.

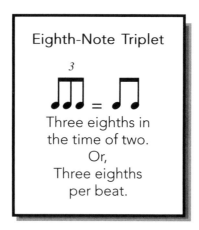

Eighth-Note Triplet

Three eighths in the time of two.
Or,
Three eighths per beat.

Count "1-&-ah, 2-&-ah," etc. as you pluck triplets in example 76A and strum them in 76B.

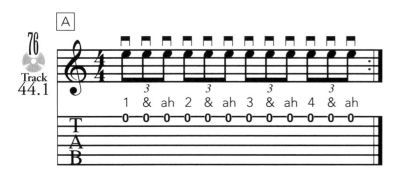

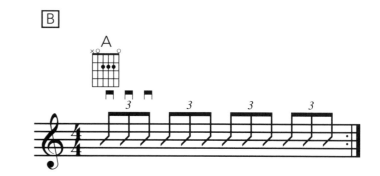

Here's a twelve-bar blues with a triplet feel. Notice the use of a "quick four" (see "Here's a Tip" on page 76).

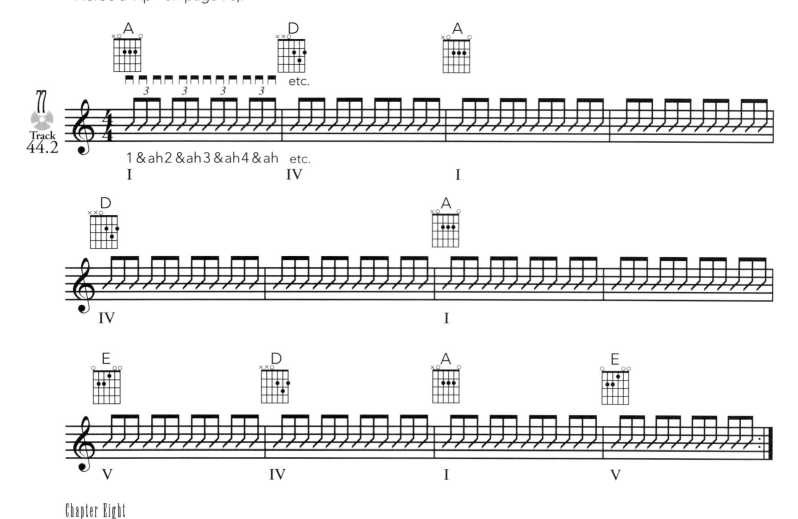

Chapter Eight

LESSON 4: SWING EIGHTH NOTES

Swing eighth notes look the same as regular eighth notes but are played differently. The first eighth note in a pair is played long (___) and the second is played short (•). It's as if the first two notes in an eighth-note triplet have been tied together.

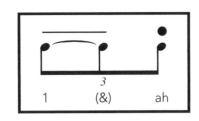

To aid in understanding the way this should sound, say "Doo Dot."

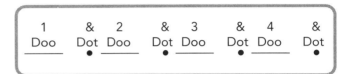

Although the eighth notes in example 77 look ordinary enough, the marking "Swing" at the beginning tells you they are anything but. Swinging eighths is not a precision art. Stay loose. Get the blues. Swing!

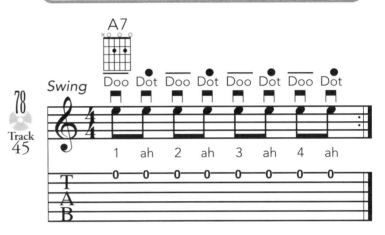

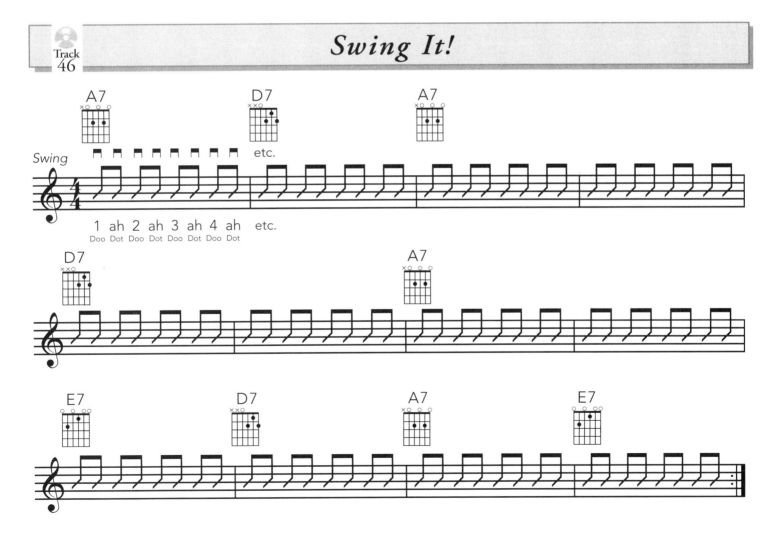

LESSON 5: BLUES PATTERN #1

Here is something you will really enjoy. Sometimes called a *shuffle pattern*, this is one of the most common and popular accompaniment figures in the blues style.

This figure can be played in place of the chords in a twelve-bar blues. Instead of strumming the chords, we strum just two strings while moving back and forth between the 1st and 3rd fingers. This works great for a blues in A.

For the A chord:
The 5th string is played open.
The 1st finger plays the 2nd fret of the 4th string and alternates with the 3rd finger, which plays the 4th fret of the 4th string.

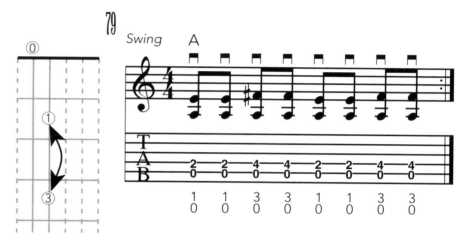

For the D chord:
The 4th string is played open.
The 1st finger plays the 2nd fret of the 3rd string and alternates with the 3rd finger, which plays the 4th fret of the 3rd string.

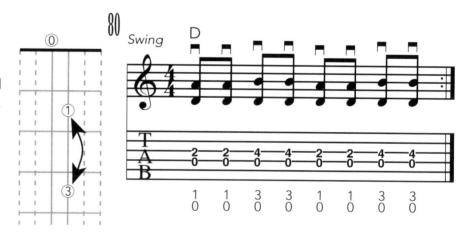

For the E chord:
The 6th string is played open.
The 1st finger plays the 2nd fret of the 5th string and alternates with the 3rd finger which plays the 4th fret of the 5th string.

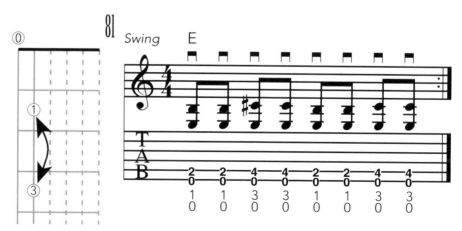

Example 81 is a classic blues-style progression using this famous accompaniment pattern. Notice that there is a move to the IV chord (D) in the second measure, as described in the tip on page 76. Also, notice that the pattern changes slightly in the twelfth measure.

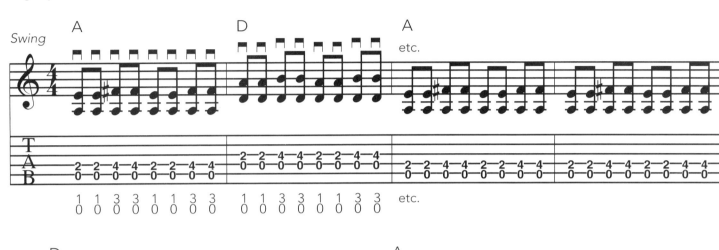

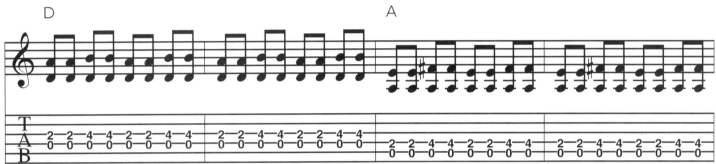

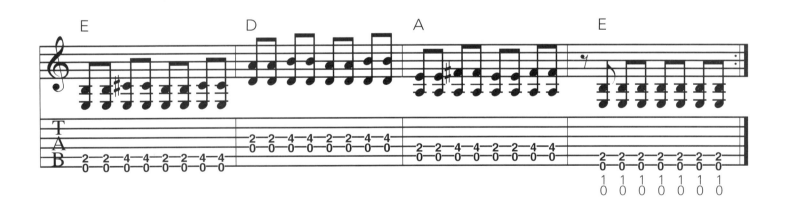

When you've got this blues tune really cookin', turn up the heat and swing the eighths! And don't forget: To bring your blues to a close, play the I chord (A)!

LESSON 6: BLUES PATTERN #2

This pattern is very similar to Pattern #1. We just add one more note to the mix. After playing the 4th fret with the 3rd finger, play the 5th fret with the 4th finger, then return to the 4th fret.

For the A chord:
The 5th string is played open.
The 1st finger plays the 2nd fret of the 4th string and then the 3rd finger plays the 4th fret of the 4th string. After that, the 4th finger plays the 5th fret of the 4th string. Finally, the 3rd finger plays the 4th fret of the 4th string again.

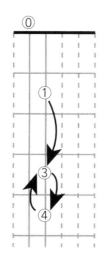
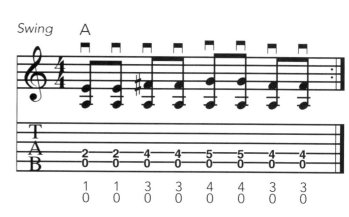

For the D chord:
The 4th string is played open.
The 1st finger plays the 2nd fret of the 3rd string and then the 3rd finger plays the 4th fret of the 3rd string. After that, the 4th finger plays the 5th fret of the 3rd string. Finally, the 3rd finger plays the 4th fret of the 3rd string again.

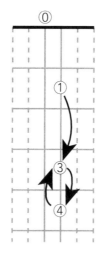
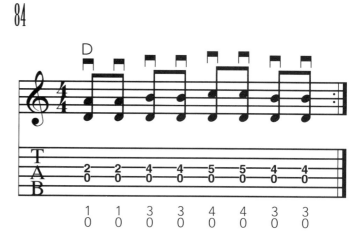

For the E chord:
The 6th string is played open.
The 1st finger plays the 2nd fret of the 5th string and then the 3rd finger plays the 4th fret of the 5th string. After that, the 4th finger plays the 5th fret of the 5th string. Finally, the 3rd finger plays the 4th fret of the 5th string again.

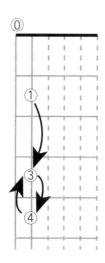
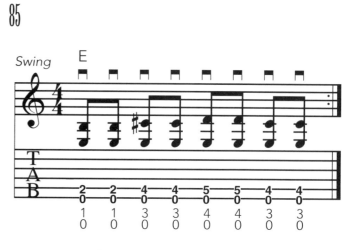

Example 85 has all the features of the music in Example 81 on page 81, but with our new blues pattern. Learn it two ways: with straight (ordinary) eighths and with swing eighths. Enjoy.

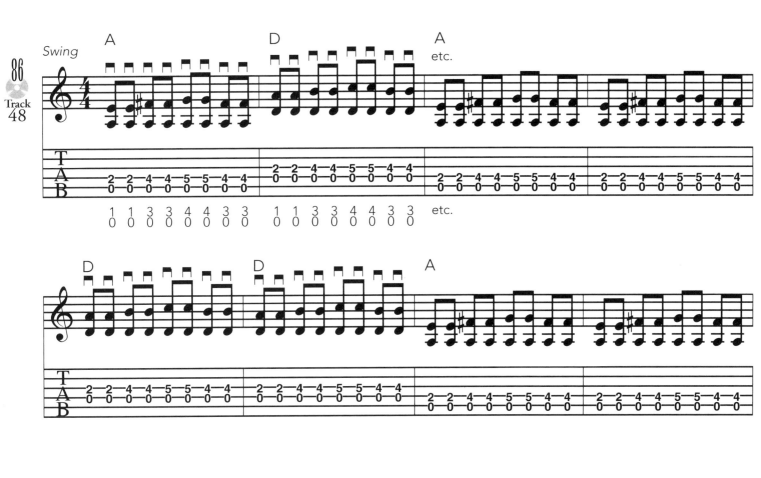

LESSON 7: A NEW BLUES RHYTHM

The simple use of an eighth-note rest and a tie from an off beat to an on beat can turn a standard twelve-bar progression into a hard-driving blues tune. Study the rhythm shown on the right. The chord is hit twice—on "1" and the "&" after "2."

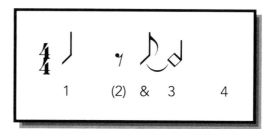

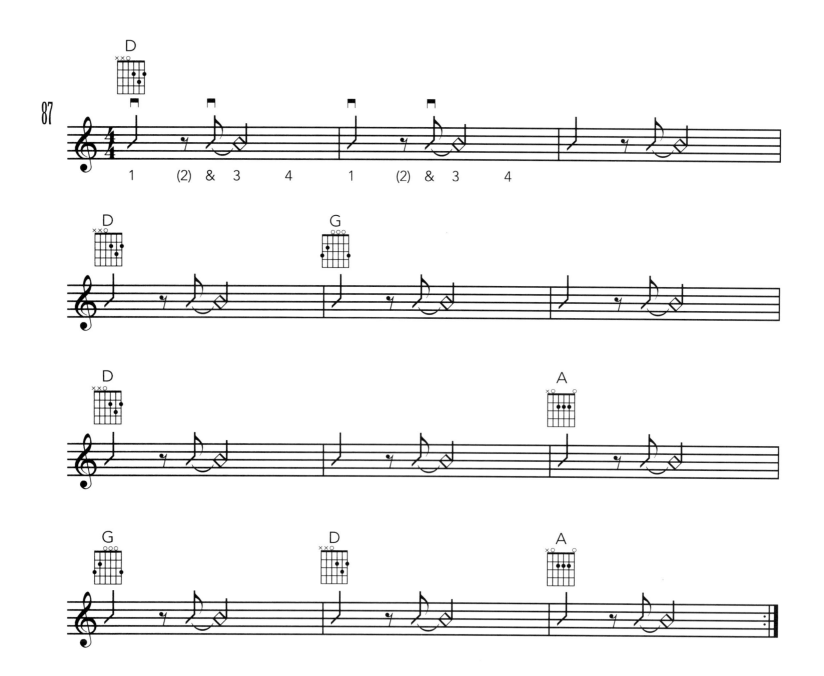

LESSON 8: A NEW CHORD—D MINOR

There's no blues like a minor blues. The sad sound of the minor chords in a blues progression, played with the right feeling, can evoke powerful emotions. Learn this simple D Minor chord and you're all set to play a minor blues in A.

Get your hanky and strum slowly but keep careful track of the bluesy rhythm.

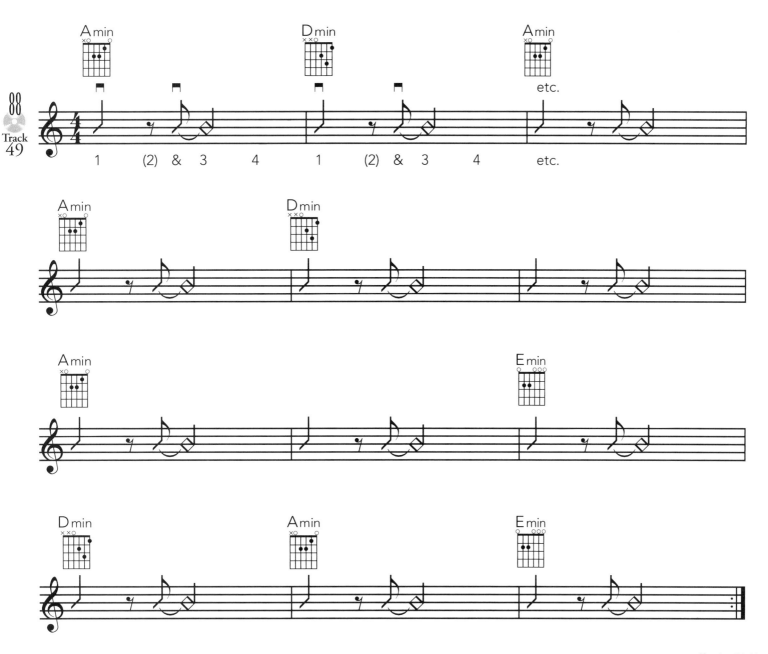

LESSON 9: A CLASSIC BLUES RIFF

Lots of blues and rock tunes are based on *riffs*. A riff is a short, repeated melodic pattern. Think back to *Crossroads* as played by Cream, *Day Tripper* by The Beatles, *Satisfaction* by The Rolling Stones—the list goes on and on. Riffs are an essential part of any guitar player's vocabulary. In this lesson, you will learn one of the most well-loved, most often-used blues riffs. Here it is:

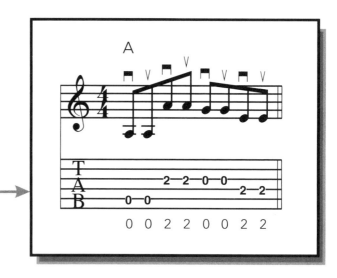

Like the blues patterns you learned on pages 80 and 82, this riff can be played in place of the chords in a twelve-bar blues in A. It works great in A because, for the I chord (A) and V chord (E), only one finger is used! Even on the IV chord (D), only two fingers are involved. Enjoy!

Here's a Tip...
This riff sounds great with swing eighth notes, too! Try it both ways: straight and swung.

Track 50

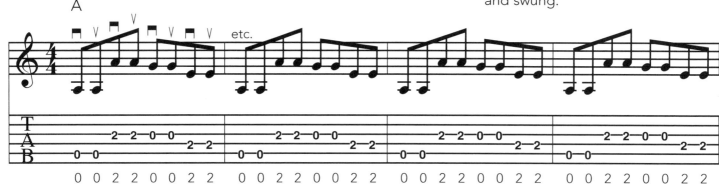

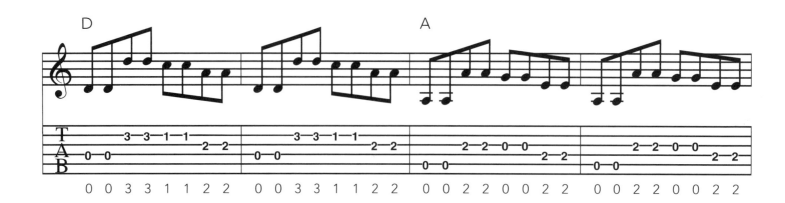

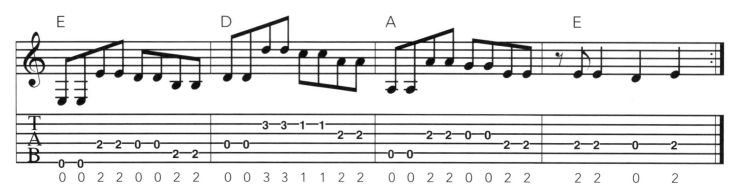

Chapter Eight

LESSON 10: A NEW CHORD—B7

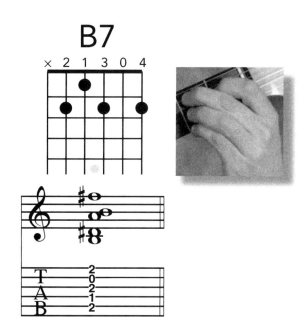

Let's be honest: All chords are not created equal. B7 is one of the tougher ones. But most people have more trouble with it than necessary. Here are two helpful tips for playing this chord:

1. Look at the shape of the notes on the 5th, 4th and 3rd strings. It's exactly the same as a D7 chord, one of your old standbys. Just add your 4th finger on the 1st string.

2. People tend to struggle with getting the 4th and 3rd fingers on the same fret without accidentally muting the 2nd string. Here's the solution: Put your 2nd finger down on its note with the thumb behind the neck and pivot by rotating your wrist at the elbow joint so that the pinky side of the hand is actually further away from the neck. Turning the hand this way makes many chords easier to play.

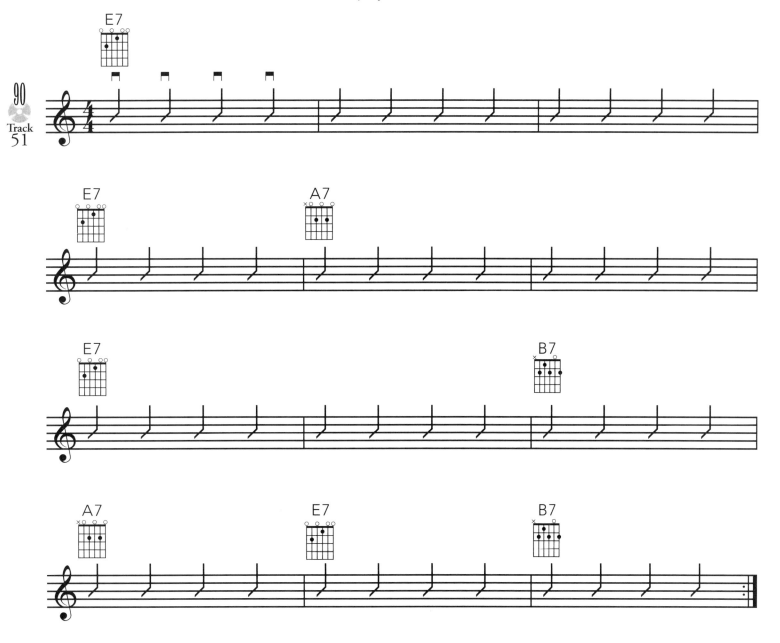

"Playing guitar has changed my life!"

LESSON 11: COOL BLUES ARTICULATION

The swing eighth-note rhythm you learned on page 79 can be given an entirely different character through the use of *articulation*. Articulation has to with the manner in which a note is performed. In this case, we will be using an articulation called *staccato*. A staccato note is played in a short, detached manner. It sounds shorter than written. For instance, a staccato quarter note will sound more like an eighth note followed by an eighth note rest.

Staccato is indicated with a dot above or below the note head. Here is a note with a staccato marking:

Play the Blues Pattern #1 (page 80) in a swing feel using staccato notes on the first note of each pair. This will give it a feel sometimes called barrelhouse swing. Enjoy!

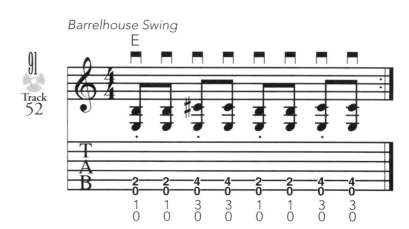

Here's a barrelhouse swing tune in the style
of Eric Clapton's *Before You Accuse Me*:

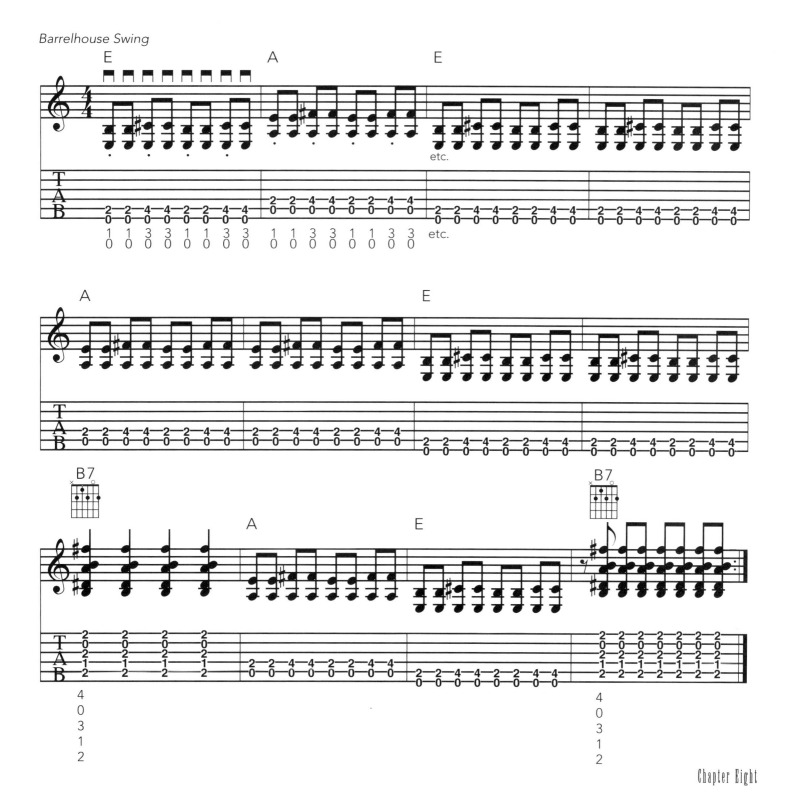

Eric's Boogie

LESSON 12: THREE MINOR 7 CHORDS—AMIN7, DMIN7 AND EMIN7

A minor blues is even bluesier when minor 7 chords (min7) are used. Play the Amin chord you learned on page 22 and alternate it with the Amin7. You will hear the difference the 7 makes. Notice that Dmin7 is just one note different than an F chord (page 52).

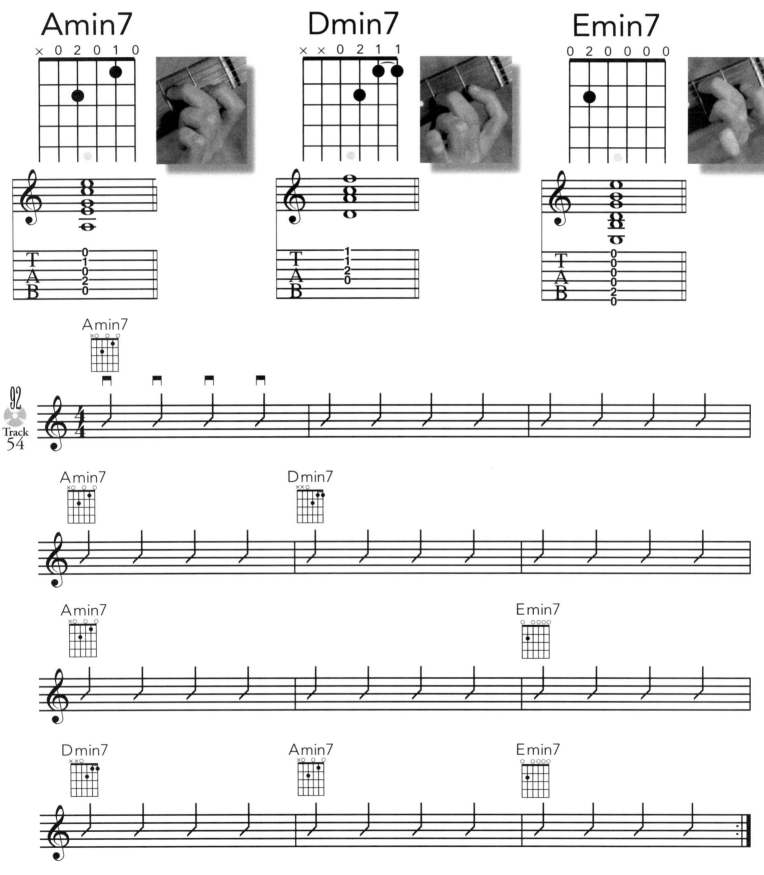

Chapter Eight

LESSON 1: MOVEABLE CHORDS

Now we really begin to move and shake as guitarists. In this one little chapter, we will expand your chord vocabulary to three times its current size.

A *moveable chord* is a chord shape that can be moved up or down the neck of the guitar. If we can identify the root contained within the chord shape and know the names of the notes (roots) along the 6th and 5th strings, we are ready to play music in any key.

The first moveable chord we will discuss is the C7 chord you learned on page 75. The root of a C7 chord, marked with an "R" in the diagram below, is located on the 5th string, 3rd fret. It is the note being held by your 3rd finger.

Because this chord contains no open strings, we can move it to anywhere on the neck and get a new chord. If we move the C7 chord up the neck one *whole step* (two frets), so that the root is on the 5th fret, we get a D7 chord. If we move the chord up one more whole step (two more frets), so that the root is on the 7th fret, we get an E7 chord.

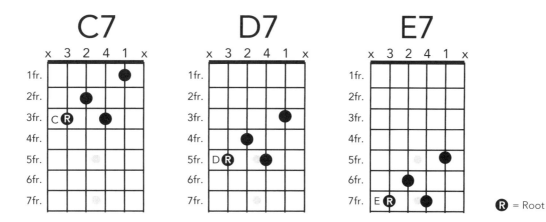

Example 92 will give you some practice moving this chord form up and down the neck.

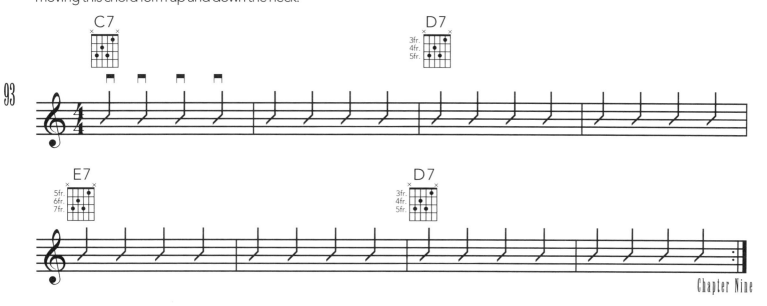

LESSON 2: ROOT-6 BARRES

The F chord (page 52) and Dmin7 chord (page 90) are both partial barre chords. They involve barreing the top two strings. The time has come to barre all six strings. While full barre chords are more physically demanding than some other chords, all guitarists eventually master them. Be patient. The rewards are many.

The first step is to place your 1st finger somewhere in the middle of the neck—such as the 5th fret—so that it covers all six strings. Apply enough pressure to make each string ring clearly. Use the thumb side of the finger and bring your elbow in closer to your side. Once this has been accomplished, you are ready for your first barre chord.

The first barre chord we will discuss is based on the E chord you learned on page 45. The root of this chord is on the 6th string, so we call barre chords based on the E chord *root-6 barres*. To play root-6 barres, we must finger the E chord differently to free up the first finger since it will make the barre. Check out the diagram below to learn the new fingering. Instead of using the 2nd, 3rd and 1st finger, use the 3rd, 4th and 2nd.

Step 1. Play the E chord with the new altered fingering. Notice that the diagram clearly marks the open 6th string, E, as the root of the chord.

Step 2. Slide your fingers up the neck (towards your body) one half step (one fret).

Step 3. Once the chord is in position, place your 1st finger across all six strings on the 1st fret. The finger now serves the same function as the open strings did in the open E chord. You are now playing an F barre chord.

Step 4. Keeping your fingers in the same shape, move your hand up one half step further. You are playing an F# barre chord.

Step 5. Repeat this process one more time, keeping the same shape and moving up the neck one more half step. Your first finger should be on the 3rd fret. You are playing a G barre chord.

> *Remember, chords that are called by just their letter names—such as "E" or "F"—are major chords.*

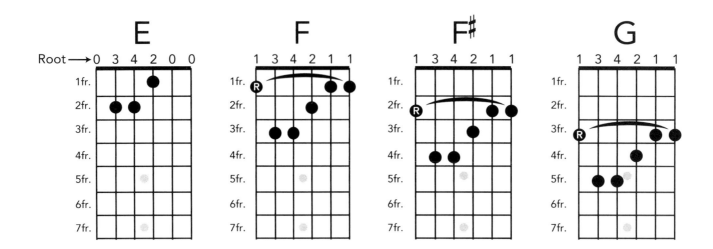

Here's a Tip...
You can do this with Emin, E7 and Emin7 too!

Follow steps 1 through 5 on page 92, strumming each chord for four measures before sliding up to the next.

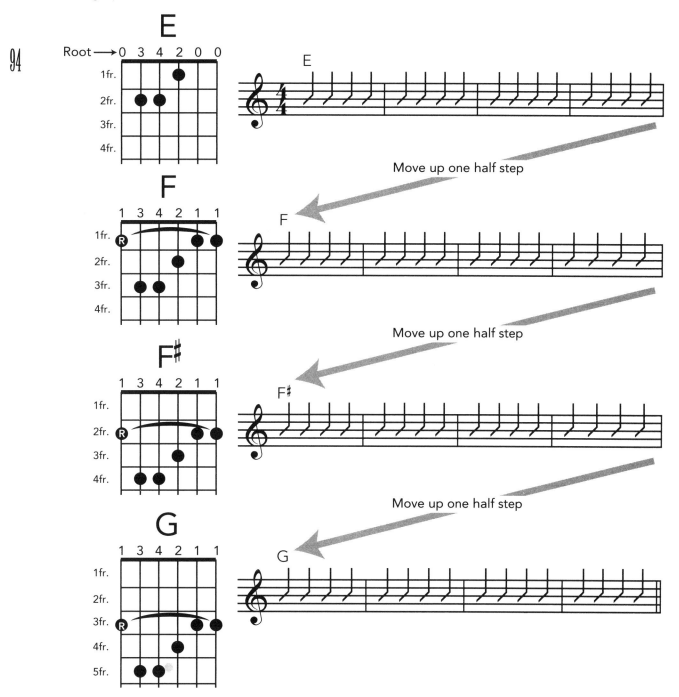

Now all you need to do is learn the names of the notes on the first twelve frets of the 6th string, and you can play *any* major chord. Here they are:

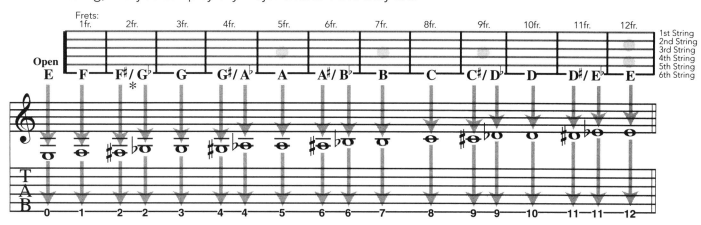

*Remember, all accidentals can be called either a sharp name or a flat name (see page 42).

Chapter Nine

LESSON 3: ROOT 5 BARRES

The procedure we applied to the E chord for creating root 6 barres can also be applied to the A chord (page 45) to create *root 5 barres*—barre chords that have the root on the 5th string. Just as for the E chord shape, we will be altering the fingering to free the 1st finger to make the barre. Check out the diagram below to learn the new fingering. Instead of using the 1st, 2nd and 3rd fingers, use the 2nd, 3rd and 4th.

Step 1. Play the A chord with the new fingering. Notice that the diagram clearly marks the open 5th string, A, as the root of the chord.

Step 2. Slide your fingers up one half step (one fret) towards your body. Place your 1st finger on the 1st fret across the first five strings. Your 1st finger is holding the root of the chord (B♭) on the 1st fret of the 5th string. You now have a B♭ barre chord.

Step 3. Keeping your fingers in the same shape, slide the chord up one half step (one fret) so that your 1st finger is on the 2nd fret, and you will have a B barre chord.

Step 4. Slide the chord up one more fret, so that your 1st finger is on the 3rd fret. You are now playing a C barre chord.

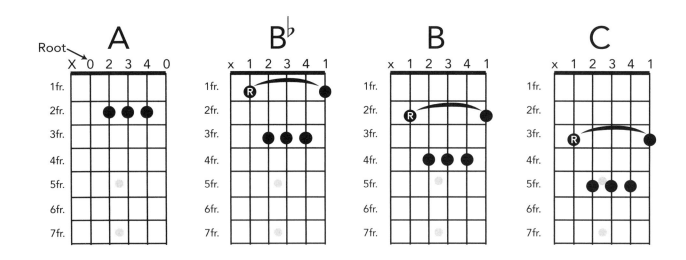

Here's a Tip...
You can do this with Amin, A7 and Amin7, too!

Here's Another Tip...
If your beefy fingers are too big to squeeze three together onto one fret, you can barre the three notes with your 3rd finger. The only disadvantage is that you will most likely mute the 1st string with the 3rd finger in the process. This is okay. Just don't barre the 1st string with the 3rd finger, too. That note doesn't belong in the chord.

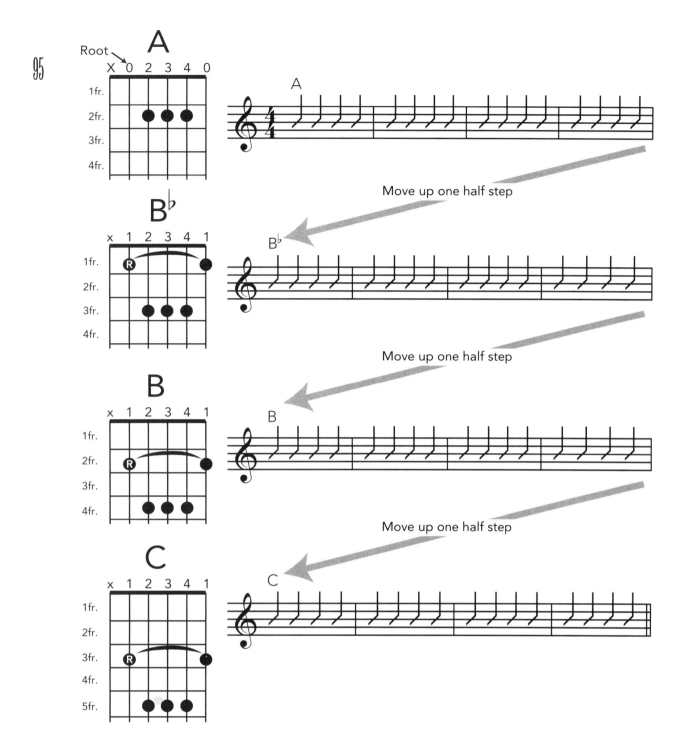

Now all you need to do is learn the names of the notes on the first twelve frets of the 5th string, and you can play any minor chord. Here they are:

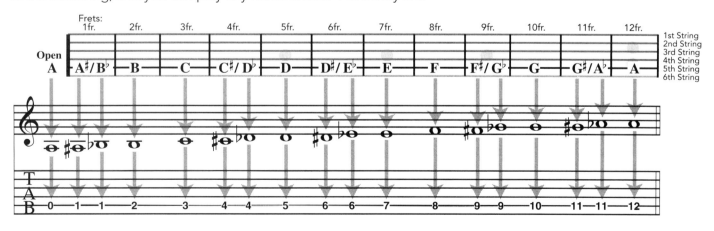

Congratulations! You have made a great start on the guitar. Don't stop now. Check out *Rock Guitar for Adults* by Tobias Hurwitz and *Blues Guitar for Adults* by Wayne Riker.